UNDERSTANDING
JIM GRIMSLEY

UNDERSTANDING CONTEMPORARY AMERICAN LITERATURE

Matthew J. Bruccoli, Founding Editor

Linda Wagner-Martin, Series Editor

UNDERSTANDING

JIM GRIMSLEY

David Deutsch

The University of South Carolina Press

Published by the University of South Carolina Press
Columbia, South Carolina 29208

www.sc.edu/uscpress

Manufactured in the United States of America

28 27 26 25 24 23 22 21 20 19 10 9 8 7 6 5 4 3 2 1

Library of Congress Cataloging-in-Publication Data
can be found at http://catalog.loc.gov/.

ISBN 978-1-61117-920-3 (hardback)
ISBN 978-1-61117-930-9 (ebook)

This book was printed on recycled paper with
30 percent postconsumer waste content

For my husband, my mother, and my father

CONTENTS

SERIES EDITOR'S PREFACE

The Understanding Contemporary American Literature series was founded by the estimable Matthew J. Bruccoli (1931–2008), who envisioned these volumes as guides or companions for students as well as good nonacademic readers, a legacy that will continue as new volumes are developed to fill in gaps among the nearly one hundred series volumes published to date and to embrace a host of new writers only now making their marks on our literature.

As Professor Bruccoli explained in his preface to the volumes he edited, because much influential contemporary literature makes special demands, "the word *understanding* in the titles was chosen deliberately. Many willing readers lack an adequate understanding of how contemporary literature works; that is, of what the author is attempting to express and the means by which it is conveyed." Aimed at fostering this understanding of good literature and good writers, the criticism and analysis in the series provide instruction in how to read certain contemporary writers—explicating their material, language, structures, themes, and perspectives— and facilitate a more profitable experience of the works under discussion.

In the twenty-first century Professor Bruccoli's prescience gives us an avenue to publish expert critiques of significant contemporary American writing. The series continues to map the literary landscape and to provide both instruction and enjoyment. Future volumes will seek to introduce new voices alongside canonized favorites, to chronicle the changing literature of our times, and to remain, as Professor Bruccoli conceived, contemporary in the best sense of the word.

Linda Wagner-Martin, Series Editor

ACKNOWLEDGMENTS

My family is filled with great readers, and I am lucky that talking over books with them is a consistent part of my life. I owe a debt of gratitude to James A. Crank for suggesting that I propose this volume to the University of South Carolina Press and to Linda Wagner-Martin and to Jim Denton at the press for agreeing to include it in their Understanding series. I would also like to thank Anna McConnell, Jacob Crawford, and Anna Hill for their invaluable help with research and fact-checking for the manuscript. Since arriving at the University of Alabama, I have been fortunate to be in a department that welcomes a robust variety of research avenues with lively discussions and collegiality and to have students here who have been eager to discuss Grimsley's work with me. I am immensely grateful both to my colleagues and to these students. An earlier version of my thoughts on *Boulevard* appeared in *LIT: Literature, Interpretation, Theory* 28.4 (2017).

CHAPTER 1

Understanding Jim Grimsley

Recalling his first experience reading *Dream Boy,* John L. Myers has reported that the "first half of the night was spent inhaling the book, for this is not the kind of novel easily read, but more drunk in. . . . The second half of the night, I sat up, alone, trying to figure out what it was I had just read."[1] By morning, Myers had concluded that he had experienced in the novel the "keen eyes of the next generation of great Southern literature."[2] Myers's assessment has been echoed by the accolades that Grimsley has gained from myriad theater patrons, reviewers, and readers. Attracting audiences both popular and scholarly, Grimsley provides a powerful, long-standing voice that insists on the socioeconomic, the sexual, and the racial diversity of the new "New South" of the late twentieth and early twenty-first centuries and on its rightfully prominent role in American literature and culture.

The South and southern social structures loom large in Grimsley's work, but his career-long investigations into rural poverty, cycles of domestic violence, a Christian-influenced spirituality, and an anticipation of powerful pleasures amid powerful pain touch chords that reach beyond region or nationality. Grimsley's earliest novels were published in Europe before a U.S. publisher took them on, although his plays have long found ready audiences in the regional urban theaters of the United States. Grimsley's widespread appeal undoubtedly has to do with what Dorothy Allison has identified as his emphasis on "choosing compassion and love, without compromising what is all too painfully known," in both literature and in life.[3] With this focus, Grimsley interrogates generally tragic circumstances and national and even international themes of economic alienation, commercial corruptions, domestic abuse, frequently repressed yet perennially present sexualities, reluctantly revised traditions, institutionalized religion, and an evolving faith in a troubled yet unrelinquished hope for self-improvement. While this analytic overview might suggest cold calculations, Grimsley presents these investigations without ever losing sight of the emotional and psychological trauma that tragic circumstances inflict on individuals and on families, the latter increasingly appearing in their modern embodiments, particularly with regard to same-sex romantic relationships. Grimsley's work draws on these situations and these relationships to evoke the complications of companionship in a carefully constructed fashion that maintains narrative swiftness without sacrificing a critical formal experimentalism. Avoiding opaqueness or an obtuse obscurity, Grimsley unfailingly shapes unusual narrative forms and styles in order to enhance the psychological and intellectual depth of his characters and to imagine how the fluidity of time and memory influences the attainment of a pragmatic, never idealized happiness.

As Grimsley's novels and plays appear with increasing frequency in bookstores, on award lists, on college syllabi, and, somewhat more slowly, in academic articles and books, it seems useful to embrace the personal, emotional, often comforting mystery that his writing provokes and simultaneously to analyze the key themes and the key aesthetic strategies engaged by his diverse body of work. Since so much of Grimsley's early writing draws from his childhood environment, a concise critical biography offers a solid first step to understanding his art.

Jim Grimsley was born on September 21, 1955, to Mary Brantham and Jasper "Jack" Grimsley, joining an older sister, Jackie, and preceding two brothers, Jasper and Brian. While Jim was born in Rocky Mount, a small town in rural eastern North Carolina, his family soon moved to Pollocksville, North Carolina, a still smaller town surrounded by narrow roads and wide fields and by the massive Croatan National Forest. The move occurred because Jasper Grimsley had taken a job as foreman on a local farm. Initially, this seemed a propitious opportunity for the family as the job came with a "somewhat respectable status" and a better pay package than one could earn driving trucks or assuming less managerial labor roles.[4] This potentially upward movement ended with a horrific reversal, however, when the elder Grimsley stuck his hand into a still-moving cornpicker and consequently lost his arm. To compound this loss, he was fired from his job as foreman and had to take work as a delivery man for a local propane company, curtailing severely the family's income. These events, Grimsley later recalled, permanently "embittered" his father, a sometimes hard worker who increasingly proved himself to be "an alcoholic, a wife-beater, and a schizophrenic descending gradually into madness," all traits that "were simply additions to the color of his reputation" for local townspeople but were the source of anxiety, fear, and outright abuse for his family.[5]

Humor, Grimsley observed, provided a bonding mechanism that helped his family to cope with his father's violence. Contemplating the "terrible things" that could happen to Grimsley when he went out that might prevent him from coming home gave the family a shared catharsis in an odd conflation of horror and relief.[6] This familial sense of the absurd echoed in a distorted fashion both the local society's and the local authorities' seeming acceptance of domestic cruelty, provided it was not taken too far, too publicly. These groups, Grimsley found, seemed to believe that men in their homes had not only the right but almost "a duty" to curtail women who "behaved badly" or who got erratically overexcited, a myopic and self-serving belief that often allowed onlookers to ignore or discount women's reports of particularly egregious brutalities.[7] Despite these hardships, Grimsley's mother stayed in her marriage in part because of the stigma attached to divorce and undoubtedly in part because of the difficulty of supporting a family on the "bit of extra money" a woman without a college education could earn, especially in Pollocksville and rural Jones County.[8] Grimsley's mother responded to these circumstances by encouraging her children to make the most of their education and to go to college so that they could obtain financial stability and independence and be able to "leave Jones County" behind.[9] Grimsley has reported, "I was lucky to have a mother who from an early age drilled into my head that I was going to college and doing something with my life."[10]

At last, though, prior to Grimsley's final year of high school, his father gave up working altogether, and his mother began to fight back decisively. Exhausted by her husband's jealous rages, his bullying, and his drug and alcohol abuse, renewed even after time spent "in an alcohol rehabilitation center," she began actively to prevent him from living with the family, remaining firm when, as Grimsley recalled, his father "attempt[ed] to return to [their] house over and over" despite being rebuffed.[11] This process led Grimsley's parents to divorce. His mother would later remarry, and Grimsley would signal his appreciation of his stepfather by thanking him in his acknowledgments to *Winter Birds* and by providing a brief portrait of him in *Comfort and Joy.* Grimsley's father, after long battles with alcoholism and mental illness, including schizophrenia, and after a substantial separation from his family, committed suicide. "I went to his funeral," Grimsley reported, "so I could see him dead," wanting to make sure that his father "was finally at some kind of state of rest that I could trust," a quietness perhaps as permanent as possible.[12] Grimsley would recount the early trauma of these years in his novels *Winter Birds* and *Comfort and Joy* and in his play *The Borderlands,* and he would draw on his need to seek visual reassurance after the death of an abuser in a powerful death scene in *My Drowning.*

As if having to survive the difficulties of Jack Grimsley's aggression, mental illness, and alcoholism were not enough, substantial medical concerns caused extra worries for the family. Jim Grimsley and his younger brother Brian had been born with hemophilia. While vital medical care created an additional expense for an already poor family, the condition also necessitated extra caution, with its attendant emotional and psychological stress, to keep both boys from getting hurt. The boys consistently had to care for their bodies and to live with a reminder of their mortality in ways that most children and young adults do not. "When I was a child," Grimsley later recalled, "the treatment for hemophilia was very bad, and not that many hemophiliacs lived beyond their teenage years. It was almost unheard of to find a hemophiliac older than thirty," a notion that engendered a persistent fear of death for decades and that seems to have made Grimsley remarkably resilient. This resiliency was essential in 1984 when he found out that he had contracted HIV. Discovering that he was HIV-positive, he remembered, was devastating and caused him to go "into therapy for a couple of years," but "after a certain point it stopped mattering so much" as he came to realize "that being on the cusp of mortality isn't that much different than being alive."[13] Both in his musing on his life and in his art, Grimsley has acknowledged the tribulations presented by his medical difficulties, but he tends to focus on being a survivor when he discusses them, and he refuses to allow his medical conditions to interrupt his attunement both to the complexity of his memories and to his perception of the potentialities of the present and the future.[14]

If learning to survive a chronic medical condition inevitably shaped Grimsley's childhood, this period was equally influenced by his initial attempts to decipher the significance of his same-sex longings amid the far-reaching sexual repressions and prejudices of his small southern town. "Our town," Grimsley recalled, "had no movie houses, no supermarkets, . . . and only one restaurant," although it "had churches in abundance, and church events ruled the calendar, with nothing but high school athletics for competition."[15] The Baptist church was an especially powerful influence in Grimsley's upbringing, his hemophilia ruling out athletics. While the church provided him with compelling stories of love, resurrection, and redemption, offering him a language and a narrative structure that he would much later reuse in his writing to offer a public exploration of the homoerotic potential of biblical stories, the institution of his church and its adherents warned a young Grimsley against acknowledging too openly any gender-nonconforming behaviors or burgeoning same-sex desires. Describing more broadly the relationship between religion and sexuality, Grimsley has remarked that the "church has reached its hand into every corner of the South," which becomes particularly problematic when it is "the church that tells us sex is nasty. . . . For gay people, this is the hardest part of all: because we can only identify ourselves as ourselves through what we desire," a traumatic identification process when institutionalized religion in much of the South signaled and uncritically still signals that same-sex desires are sinful and alienating. Of course, Grimsley has noted, expressions of queer sexualities certainly existed in the rural South of the 1960s, despite their being taboo, but they were often gossiped about through coded references to strange, odd, or crazy individuals, references that indicated a clear public disapproval of even consensual same-sex sexual relationships.[16]

In Grimsley's unfortunately far from unique case, mutually influential church and gossipy rhetorical practices filtered into subtler schoolroom insinuations. Grimsley recalled that, with his "slightly effeminate way of speaking and moving," he was early on labeled a sissy and that by elementary school his classmates had "started to move beyond calling [him] a sissy to hint that [he] might be something worse," presumably gay.[17] In these cases, elementary school insinuations imitated church and social gossip, condemning boys who deviated too far from conventional gender or sexual practices as being supposedly worse than those who adhered to them. Still, Grimsley has reported that he had little trouble with overt homophobia, in part because he had numerous female friends, both black and white, in part because he was good at dancing, which made him popular, and in part because of his hemophilia, which kept people from bullying him because of how easily he could be seriously hurt. Most of all, however, he remembers that he was protected from excessively severe social reprisals because by the mid- to late 1960s "the social core" of his school had been largely dismantled by the enormous upheaval caused by enforced integration in the South.[18] In the turmoil of integration and the flight of wealthier white students to private institutions, he was allowed at school the pretense that he had "no interest in love" one way or another.[19] The seismic social shock of integration thus allowed Grimsley to put off fully coming to terms with his sexuality in private or in public until he left Pollocksville.

If his sexuality remained largely unexamined, integration did cause Grimsley to reevaluate, albeit cautiously, both the spoken and the unspoken racial taboos in his environment and to observe the power of minority resiliency in the face of reactionary politics and social customs. When the federal government forced Jones County to combine black and white public school populations, in 1966, Grimsley witnessed increasing cracks in his environment's normalization of white supremacy and legalized segregation. His new black classmates and his own burgeoning willingness to engage in self-critique challenged the social training that had led him by the age of eleven to be what he has described as "a good little racist," one prepared to insult and degrade his new classmates, who responded by standing their ground, remaining "defiantly proud of themselves" despite harassment and threatening insults.[20] As the years passed, Grimsley gradually became friendly with several black students, whom he still continued to think of as "not as good as I was," although, as he found his black classmates to be intelligent and affable, his lived experience ended up "colliding with [his] upbringing."[21] This collision forced him to reassess, if all too slowly, his understanding of race relations, especially in the reshaped schools, which, as he recollected, were for black students "no longer a haven from prejudice but . . . rather a study in it" as white teachers and students regularly denied them "equal status."[22] In his memoir *How I Shed My Skin: Unlearning the Racist Lessons of a Southern Childhood* (2015), his insightful reconsideration of his own evolving racial ideologies, Grimsley emphasizes the slowness of his recognition of the way in which racial politics work and the unfortunate tendency for the oppression of one minority to prove beneficial to another, as, for example, the tensions arising from integration distracted from consideration of his queerness in Jones County schools. It was not until college, Grimsley has reported, that he grew more actively critical of his place as a white, queer man from a working-class family in the South as he "became aware of black political movements, and [his] own coming out as a gay person began to educate [him] in the mechanics of oppression."[23] As the years passed, Grimsley would come to realize and to emphasize in his fiction the interconnected nature of diverse forms of oppression.

Indeed, from the perspective of a critical biographical approach to Grimsley's writing, perhaps the most useful part of *How I Shed My Skin* is its revelation of how attentive the older Grimsley worked to be to the subtly informative and often intimately interconnected coercions of the daily environments that formed him. Careful to avoid homogenizing his region and its inhabitants, in his memoir Grimsley focused on integration in his specific "place in the South," but he did so to critique the pervasive "mechanics of oppression" that Jones County shared with much of the United States and to demonstrate how subtle yet widespread tropes of homophobia and racism can intersect with each other and with misogyny and classism not only overtly but as part of what he calls a "silent system" or a "quiet set of rules," such as those adhered to if not always articulated by those around him in his childhood.[24] If racial differences, for instance, shaped in part by the patriarchal socioeconomic disparities of American capitalism, came to the fore in Grimsley's schools, these problems also lingered, festering in the background landscape. The farm in Pollocksville where Grimsley's father had worked and from which he had been let go was "a remnant of an old plantation," and the town was dotted with the decay of impoverished small-town America, old houses falling down and left to rot beside a "mobile home" or "a new cinderblock house" situated amid "old appliances and rusted cars."[25] Taking a broader yet generally accurate perspective, Grimsley has noted that in the rural South "we have the past rotting beside the present, in town and out of town."[26] Part of this multifaceted past, often uncritiqued and overlooked by the white population, were the lingering visual signs of intolerant ideologies and a reluctance or a downright refusal to change that worked in conjunction with and even embraced the casual acceptance of aggressive economic and educational inequality, greed, racism, and misogyny, evidenced by rot kept alongside scarcely better if newer living conditions and uses of the epithets "nigger" or "sissy" in intensely demeaning quotidian contexts. These everyday economic gaps, the racist remarks, and the derision aimed at effeminate men and women, Grimsley has consistently suggested, formed an interconnected "silent system," one interwoven with a pervasive sexual repression that made even the landscape of daily family life an often tacit battleground that was particularly difficult for queer individuals.[27]

Widespread institutional manias and repressions in these ways shaped particular families and individual lives. This intermingling of public and private, as Grimsley has analyzed it, at times led to a kind of insanity for unconventional individuals, one that blurred any clearcut distinctions between imagined or literary tropes and everyday experiences in the rural South. Consequently, as Grimsley has noted, "in the South, the family is a field where craziness grows like weeds," and he has described how his family grew up in "the land of Southern gothic" as "heirs to Southern darkness" or at least to a particular strain of it.[28] While these might seem like quaint colloquial phrasings, such an interpretation belies the pain, the suffering, and the psychological scarring that so many institutionally endorsed repressions both support and condone. Grimsley's autobiographical memories of a disjunction between kindness and cruelty and of a nostalgia for an often welcoming rural or small-town environment that mixes with memories of virulent hatred and fear, poverty, and daily disenfranchisements of women, people of color, and sexual or gender nonconformists are reminders that terms such as "southern gothic" and their analogues are more than just clichéd literary tropes. They are heuristic devices for understanding a version of the South, even of the United States, in which people lived and made their homes and that still exists very much alive around us.

Grimsley's memories of his childhood and of Jones County of course stayed with him, haunting and inspiring him, after he graduated from high school and went on to college at the University of North Carolina at Chapel Hill. At UNC Grimsley studied creative writing with Max Steele and Doris Betts, which, as Chris Freeman has noted, put him "in the company of some of the most successful southern writers," and in this environment Grimsley began to draw on his past to construct what would eventually become *Winter Birds*.[29] It would take more than a decade, however, for him to achieve publication and a career as an author. After graduating college with honors, in 1978, Grimsley left North Carolina and found work variously at a "liquor store" and taking "phone orders for sanitary maintenance supplies in New Orleans," while living for a while in "an apartment on Dumaine Street," only steps from the city's night life.[30] Here he got to experience the increasing vitality of queer life in the late-1970s French Quarter and its environs, which would provide inspiration most notably for his play *Mr. Universe* and for his novel *Boulevard*. Grimsley has recalled how he "lived near many gay men in the French Quarter" and spent time cruising the "French Quarter bars," which were "so consumed with sex" that he found himself "terrified most of the time, awaiting the wrath of God," having "taken the lies about Jesus too far into [his] bones" so that he still "smelled sin everywhere."[31] Having escaped the domineering order of the Baptist calendar in Pollocksville, he could not quite overcome his childhood church's homophobic lessons or its "silent system" of repression. As such, he mistook the smell of the French Quarter's filth and refuse, mixed in with its erotic glamour and excitement, for sexual sin.

In subsequent years, Grimsley would shift from battling the "lies" told about Jesus by church institutions to focusing on a more balanced, spiritual version of Christian narratives. In his novels, for instance, he would emphasize the "kind of comfort" that he found in Christian stories and depict the protection that queer individuals and characters might find in a spiritual if not always a human-run institutional Christianity. This protection reflects the shelter that Grimsley himself had found in his church when young, despite its public insistence on the "nastiness" of sex and its teaching of an aggressive patriarchy in which men are taught to marry and then to "rule over women."[32] This balanced and complicated engagement with a spiritual Christianity that promises love and life after sacrifice and its intermingling with violent institutional perversions of these promises is one that Grimsley would explore in particular depth in *Dream Boy*, in *Comfort and Joy*, and to an equally complicated degree in his fantasy and science fiction novels.

In 1980, Grimsley decided to leave New Orleans, and he moved to Atlanta, where he found work in various clerical roles at Grady Hospital and where he began to gain increasing recognition in the theatrical and publishing worlds, which eventually led, in 1999, to his joining the Creative Writing faculty at Emory University, where he still teaches.[33] In addition to offering long-term work in more professional contexts, Atlanta provided Grimsley with a more politically aware and more socially liberating home. Choosing to live in Atlanta's Little Five Points, "a famous lesbian neighborhood," Grimsley made friends and established associations with lesbians and free, "independent" women, women who facilitated what he has called his "long education in what it means to be homosexual." In the "early 1980s," as he pointed out, "we gay people were at the beginning of a cycle of years that would lead us to a greater visibility, if, alas, not a greater unity, than we had ever before enjoyed," and Atlanta, with its queer bars, organizations, artists, and summer "Gay Pride" weekends, was a focal point for this visibility in the South, vitally so after the devastating appearance of AIDS.[34] If queer communities, as Grimsley acknowledged, were still too often segregated according to sex, color, and, frequently, socioeconomic class, Atlanta provided one metropolitan point of organized and informal crossovers that indicated frequent, if at times skeptical, attempts to find freedom and self-worth in a region historically linked to racial, gendered, and sexual oppressions.[35]

In Atlanta, Grimsley's personal development grew apace with his writing as this invigorating if still problematic urban environment provided him with welcoming and encouraging audiences. While supporting himself financially through his work at Grady, Grimsley experienced his first sustained artistic successes in Atlanta theaters, beginning with *The Existentialists,* produced in 1983 at Atlanta's ACME theater, and *The Earthlings,* produced in 1984 at Little Five Point's 7 Stages theater, co-founded by Del Hamilton and Faye Allen, who would become Grimsley's long-term professional and personal associates. Fourteen of Grimsley's plays, by Wendell Ricketts's count, "were produced between 1983 and 1993," and in 1986 Grimsley became the playwright-in-residence at 7 Stages, which led to the production of his *Mr. Universe* in 1987.[36] Curt Holman has noted that "Grimsley completed the play in 1986 while performing in 7 Stages' production of Sam Shepard's *The Tooth of Crime*" and that *Mr. Universe* served as the "inaugural production" for the theater company's new Euclid Avenue building.[37] While several of Grimsley's themes of unconventional self-invention and self-promotion amid violence resonate with Shepard's *The Tooth, Mr. Universe* develops its own material by considering these themes in terms of drag queens, violence, and the self-fashioning of a developing queer culture in 1970s New Orleans. The play was, Grimsley remembered, his first hit; it would be restaged again in Atlanta and elsewhere across the United States, and it provided the title for Grimsley's only collection of drama to date, *Mr. Universe and Other Plays,* published in 1998.[38] In the meantime, Grimsley's work as a dramatist earned him well-deserved critical acclaim, including the 1988 Newsday's George Oppenheimer award for the Best New American Playwright and the 1993 Bryan Family Foundation Award for Drama. As Grimsley's career progressed, he became known more for his novels than for his plays, although in 2009 he remarked, "Some people think I'm a novelist dabbling in the art form, and that's not true at all," a fact evidenced by his long and continuing history with the theater, even if the vast majority of his professionally performed plays have not yet been published.[39]

While enjoying success as a dramatist in the 1980s, Grimsley continued to write prose. He had a stand-alone short story, "City and Park," published in *Carolina Quarterly* and quickly republished in Houghton Mifflin's *Best American Short Stories of 1982* and, later, in his own 2008 collection, *Jesus Is Sending You This Message,* and he carefully refined and persistently sent out for review what would become *Winter Birds.* After finishing *Winter Birds,* in 1984, he had immense difficulty in finding a publisher for it in part because of its unconventional second-person perspective and in part because of its sad narrative trajectory.[40] Believing in the book despite rejections, Grimsley found his persistence rewarded when the German publisher Zebra, under the guidance of Frank Heibert, finally published *Winter Birds* as *Wintervögel* in 1992, leading to a string of publishing successes.[41] The French publisher Éditions Métailié brought out the novel in 1994 as *Les oiseaux de l'hiver,* which won Grimsley the Prix Charles Brisset in the same year. In addition, 1994 saw a third publication of *Winter Birds,* this time in English, by Algonquin, which had initially refused the manuscript in 1985. The second time around, Algonquin sent the novel to Dorothy Allison for evaluation, and she reported back, "I loved this book as if it were my own."[42] Allison's positive review sparked a mutually beneficial relationship between Grimsley and Algonquin that would endure through the publications of all Grimsley's early novels in English. In the short term, Grimsley's at-long-last English edition of *Winter Birds* earned him the Sue Kaufman Prize for First Fiction in 1995 and a position as a finalist for the PEN/Hemingway Award.[43]

In 1995 Algonquin also published Grimsley's *Dream Boy,* which in 1996 won the American Library Association's Gay, Lesbian, and Bisexual Book Award. Positive reviews appeared in venues such as the *Harvard Gay & Lesbian Review,* where Chris Freeman characterized the novel as "both tragic and triumphant," an extension of the tradition established by E. M. Forster's *Maurice,* as both works depict couples that "carved out new, resistant spaces for themselves so that their love [could] continue," and in the *Chicago Review,* where David Ebershoff observed, "Grimsley has written a fresh and beautiful book."[44] Eric Rosen adapted the novel into a play that premiered in 1996 at Chicago's About Face Theater and that he revived in 1998 in Atlanta and in Chicago, continuing a long-standing partnership that would lead to Grimsley's selection as About Face Theater's playwright-in-residence from the 1999–2000 season until 2004.[45] In 2008 James Bolton adapted *Dream Boy* for a fairly faithful film, which was selected for screening at the Berlin International Film Festival. In 1997 Grimsley went on to publish *My Drowning,* which won him his first Georgia Author of the Year Award, in 1998, and which, along with his previous writings, won him a Lila Wallace–Reader's Digest Writers' Award. Grimsley finished this tremendous decade with the publication in English in 1999 of *Comfort and Joy,* part of which had already appeared in *Men on Men 6* and which as a novel had been published in Dutch, German, and French.[46] In English, it was a finalist for the American Library Association's (by this time more inclusively named) Gay, Lesbian, Bisexual, and Transgende[r] Book Award.

In the early twenty-first century, Grimsley branched out and published longer works in the fantasy and science fiction genres as well as novels set in urban environments, settings previously found primarily in his drama. In 2000 he published *Kirith Kirin,* the first of a series of interconnected and yet standalone narratives, which extended to *The Ordinary* in 2004 and to *The Last Green Tree* in 2006. The first two novels won Lambda awards for Gay and Lesbian Science Fiction, Fantasy, and Horror in 2001 and 2005, respectively. Stories related to the series have appeared in *The Year's Best Science Fiction,* volumes 16 and 19, and fairly regularly in the magazine *Asimov's Science Fiction* from 2001 until 2015. Interspersed with his fantasy and science fiction work, Grimsley returned to a New Orleans setting in 2002 for *Boulevard,* from which an excerpt had previously appeared in *Men on Men 2000;* the novel won him his second Georgia Author of the Year Award, in 2003. Grimsley's profuse, diverse, and consistently high-quality creative production won him an award in literature from the American Academy of Arts and Letters in 2005. Never one to rest on his laurels, Grimsley shortly published his next urban- and suburban-centered novel, *Forgiveness,* in 2006; his short-story collection, *Jesus Is Sending You This Message,* in 2008; and, in 2015, his memoir, *How I Shed My Skin,* which he wrote with what Randall Kenan has described as "skill and delicacy."[47]

How I Shed My Skin provides fascinating reading because of its attention to history presented in a strategic style to evoke how a naïve child could learn to consider competing narratives and to evolve thereby into a more critically thinking adult. In doing so, it also evidences how an understanding of Grimsley's personal history can enhance an understanding of his particular interventions, thematically and stylistically, into a larger literary context. In much of his writing, Grimsley considers the interconnected mechanics of domestic abuse, misogyny, classism, greed, homophobia, and racism, as well as ways to counter these mechanics, in a fashion that expands and redefines the bounds not just of southern but of American literary traditions. In 1980, Richard King observed that reading William Faulkner had helped him to realize that "the final definition of 'being Southern' had not been established," and literary scholars such as Trudier Harris, Patricia Yaeger, and James A. Crank, among others, have continued to turn us toward the vital if too often marginalized narratives that emphasize the multifaceted and intersecting identities of southern African Americans, women, and same-sex-desiring individuals, to name just a few identities relevant to Grimsley's work.[48] These scholars take part in a long-standing endeavor to challenge, refine, and contest any narrow or finalized definition of "being Southern" or of southern literature, itself of course part and parcel of being American and of American literature. Grimsley's writing works hand in hand with this endeavor, particularly in his attention to the experiences, fictional and nonfictional, of growing up gay, not quite conventionally masculine, and poor in rural North Carolina and then transitioning to the differently structured opportunities of cities such as New Orleans and Atlanta.

Grimsley has himself several times highlighted the importance of these autobiographical elements to his path-breaking early fiction. With regard to *Winter Birds* he has observed, "What I have written is autobiographical but is not an autobiography" or an entirely accurate retelling of past events.[49] Elsewhere, he observed that "in *Winter Birds* it's all fiction, even though it's based in fact," while, analogously, *My Drowning* is "based on [his] mother's childhood" and family stories. In reaction to queries about about the autobiographical nature of *My Drowning*, Grimsley himself has pointed out that he was obviously never a "nineteen-year-old girl," an observation that extends to any of the female characters whom he depicts, including a same-sex female couple.[50] His drive to create "fiction . . . based in fact," however, encouraged Grimsley to expand what he saw as the thematic limitations of twentieth-century American queer fiction. "Too much of early gay literature," he has argued, "has been concerned with beautiful, rich, white, gay men in the bars and gay ghettoes" and consequently has depicted only a small slice of "what gay life is really like in this country."[51] In 1999 Grimsley again noted that the "majority of gay novels are about urban settings, and they're not about adolescents. What's out there now is a Northeastern, prep school point of view. It was never about my life. . . . And gay novels are not very often about relationships, and until *Bastard Out of Carolina* by Dorothy Allison [1992] came along, there were none set in the South."[52] Grimsley's attention to a multifaceted South has allowed him to critique the particular values of what Kaye Gibbons has called his "southern citizens," and he has often paid particular attention to depicting queer characters as uniquely shaped individuals with subtle complexities developed from the variations of southern history, culture, and life from modern Atlanta to historic Savannah and New Orleans to the devastating hardships of impoverished families struggling in the eastern tobacco country in North Carolina.[53] As such, *Winter Birds,* which has subtle if pointed homoerotic passages, *Dream*

Boy, Comfort and Joy, and significant sections of *My Drowning* have worked to shift the sexual, gendered, socioeconomic, and geographical centers of both southern fiction and queer fiction and consequently of American fiction more broadly.

Having acknowledged this shift, we should note that while Grimsley's critique regarding the "majority of gay novels" is generally accurate, a more nuanced perspective of queer southern literature is useful for understanding his remarkable achievement in expanding the perspectives of turn-of-the-twenty-first-century American fiction and for understanding his place within its established traditions. Grimsley's critique of "gay novels" is somewhat polemical and might be considered a reaction against what Scott Herring has called a queer "U.S. metronormativity," a perspective or style composed of an urbane "cosmopolitanism, sophistication, knowingness, refinement, worldliness, and trendy fashion" influenced most often by metropolitan environments, especially New York City.[54] In many cases, this northeastern metronormativity is misleading considering that the U.S. South has, as Gary Richards once remarked, "persisted in contributing some of the nation's foremost gay authors," and it has thus led to frustration for authors, readers, and critics interested in more regional or even rural queer settings and identities and the stories that have developed from them.[55] Grimsley works largely, although not entirely, within these latter traditions, and his early novelistic themes, despite his more explicit style of writing about sex and sexuality, should be linked to the queer rural identities and relationships intimated, if not always overtly discussed or defined, in Thomas Hal Phillips's *The Bitterweed Path* (1949), in William Goyen's *The House of Breath* (1950), and in Tennessee Williams's *Cat on a Hot Tin Roof* (1955). Grimsley's work should also be read in the context of more contemporary works such as John Rechy's *City of Night* (1963), which centers on poor hustlers; Randall Kenan's *A Visitation of Spirits* (1989) and *Let the Dead Bury Their Dead* (1992), which center on small-town African American communities; and Dorothy Allison's *Trash* (1988) or *Bastard Out of Carolina* (1992), which center on relationships between women in poor southern settings.

Michael Bibler, E. Patrick Johnson, John Howard, William Mark Poteet, Gary Richards, and Mab Segrest, among others, have done groundbreaking work to uncover and to trace the literary lineage of such queer elements in southern art and life and to ascertain how queerness exists within the myriad intersecting identities of diverse southern communities, such as those explored in fiction by Kenan and Allison.[56] Accounting for these literary predecessors and contemporaries of Grimsley and their concern with queer sexual identities that must negotiate rural poverty, family, racial tension, violence, faith, and myriad social stigmas can help readers to understand Grimsley's place in a larger tradition as well as his desire to bring these concerns closer to the fore in cultural conversations. As this volume shows, such queer intersections are woven into much of Grimsley's writing, and if Grimsley has at times admirably embraced critics' occasional categorization of him as a "gay writer"—he once remarked, "I'm proud to be known as that. It puts me with some wonderful company"—he has consistently made sure to develop this one identifying element through complex depictions of multifaceted characters and experiences.[57] As such, Grimsley's work, so often a finely wrought and historically conscious fictionalization of southern times, places, and cultures, with his special attention to queer individuals who live in and survive rural poverty and abuse, who find in religion both an enemy and a legitimation for queer love, and who find connections among the mechanics of U.S. oppressions of queerness, women, and people of color, should add valuably to both recent critical investigations into and an expanding interest in queer rural life.

Any focus, however, on Grimsley's historically conscious autobiographical settings and themes should not distract from the careful style and form with which he imbues his work, even as the former has overtly influenced the latter. Most apparently, Grimsley weaves into his writing lyrics from Christian hymns and carols and the redemptive structures of biblical stories from his youth, fashioning these into legitimations of and supports for same-sex love. Signaling additional influences, he has recalled how in his childhood his hemophilia forced him to spend long stretches of time healing in bed, periods when he spent "hours reading comic books and classic adventure stories like Edgar Rice Burroughs's Tarzan books," as well as books by Robert A. Heinlein, P. L. Travers, and Madeleine L'Engle.[58] Traces of these stylistic influences can be found in Grimsley's own fiction, from fantastical descriptions of Danny's adventures in a forest with the River Man in *Winter Birds* to the surrealistic elements of *Dream Boy* to technical descriptions of time travel and the creation of alien technology and words in his own fantasy and science fiction. In a vein similarly concerned with exoticism and time, Grimsley's novels and plays also draw on southern gothic stylizations. He employs descriptions of the past decaying in the present in the form of rotting plantation wealth or impoverished tenant farmers' homes, of southern foliage, and of graveyards and ghosts, quasi-supernatural or grotesque scenes reminiscent of those from his childhood and those fashioned by William Faulkner and Tennessee Williams, although Grimsley uses passages in this style more sparingly to create his own haunting, retrospective movement forward as his characters consistently flee these unforgettable spaces.

At times Grimsley has welcomed loose comparisons between his work and that of such canonically southern authors even as his trimmer, less reiterative style, and sparser dialogue differ from Faulkner's extensive play with language and recursivity or from Williams's ornate flourishes and soliloquies. As Grimsley has noted, he accepts these comparisons partly for pragmatic reasons, because "Southern literature gets talked about," but also because they fit, since much of what he writes "sounds Southern in terms of word choice and diction," so a linguistically or semantically southern style in his writing seems inescapable, although his use of neologisms and world-making in his fantasy and science fiction prevent any broadly comprehensive claims for his overarching southern-ness. Still, to contextualize Grimsley's aesthetic properly, it is useful to note his engagement through his wide reading and his theatrical career with the experimental surrealism of Sam Shepard, his admiration for the sensitively symbolic plays of María Fornés and Pearl Cleage, and the lyrical, often enigmatic qualities, what Grimsley has called the compressed, "denser and richer than usual" writing, of Nathanael West or Virginia Woolf and the "wonderful crypticness" that emerges through the still incredibly specific writing in Djuna Barnes's *Nightwood* (1936).[59] As these stylistic influences on Grimsley's thinking suggest, his writing cannot be easily characterized or contained by generalized references to the South or to southern literature because, if rooted in the diverse terrains of the South, his work extends and enriches a truly cosmopolitan array of literary lineages.

Simultaneously, always reimagining and never imitating, Grimsley translates much of his fictional influences into styles and forms all his own, if ones that vary tremendously from piece to piece. Writing his novels from diverse points of view, from the second-person present tense in *Winter Birds* to variations between the third-person past tense and the first-person present tense in *Boulevard,* and merging formal English with slang terms and dialects in dramas such as *Mr. Universe* and in novels such as *My Drowning,* Grimsley carefully matches his style and form to the mood or vision that he wants to evoke.[60] Indeed, Grimsley's work frequently recalls his own praise of Flannery O'Connor, who, he observed, was able to take "a fairly simple situation and complicate it and complicate it," or of Ford Madox Ford, who could create a "pristine voice . . . very civilized but full of danger all the way through."[61] Grimsley too manages to take a simple situation, such as the appearance of a mute stranger in *Mr. Universe* or a university photographer wanting to take pictures of a rural house in *Winter Birds* or the recurrence of folklore in *My Drowning,* and reveal its pleasures and violence as considered by a character at different ages, after different experiences, and in different iterations of remembering.

The variety of voices and forms that it takes to present these complexities, to achieve the balance between revealing the civilizing and the violent tendencies of such situations, is evidence of Grimsley's own mastery over a plenitude of structural variations. Admiring Hemingway as "an extraordinary stylist,"

Grimsley has pointed out that the older author "does become predictable and repeatable in some of what he's written, and I don't want that to be true of me."[62] If recurrent interests in the fluidity of time, history, gender, abuse, greed, scarcity, and queerness emerge throughout Grimsley's career, his writing is certainly not predictable or dull, and reviewers have generally reacted well to his stylistic and formal experiments, frequently praising the language he uses to construct them. What Drew Limsky has called "florid," David Ebershoff has recognized as subtle and Fred Chappell has described, perhaps most aptly, as "taut but delicate writing."[63] While Grimsley's style transformed as he pursued thematic innovations in each new novel or play, his attention to subtle suggestiveness and to a seeming simplicity that blooms into complexity, together with an avoidance of any heavy-handed didacticism, held true to his early observation that "to do a thing subtly is always more powerful—always—than to really do it full out. To stop just short of doing it, so that the finishing of the gesture is in your hand, the reader."[64] This narrative restraint helps to explain Grimsley's eschewal of overt explanation, his skilled use of ellipses and italics to intimate memories recalled in the present tense that provide fragments of narrative for reflection but that also mute the pain of sustained abuse. It also helps to describe his use of strategic sexual explicitness, always brief and never gratuitous, that veers from pragmatic descriptions of having safe sex in *Comfort and Joy* to more dangerous erotic encounters in New Orleans. As these examples indicate, Grimsley creates a new style, a new form for each piece of writing.

In recent years, Grimsley has expanded his formal experimentations still further to account for the pervasiveness of twenty-four-hour news shows that masquerade as substantive journalism and of more overtly commercial media, often transmitted through devices that allow for the shallowest of engagements with watershed political and social moments. This comes through in his use of typographically distinctive short news flashes in *The Last Green Tree*, provided by devices that recall the smartphones of the early twenty-first century and in his parodies of television talk show interviews and the surrealism of car commercials in his acerbic satire *Forgiveness*. These examples indicate how as ways of constructing narratives multiply in our modern world, Grimsley adapts them to his fiction, always with a sensitive yet never sentimentally nostalgic consciousness of the past. Grimsley's consistently insightful treatments of both taboo and popular topics of conversation combined with his stylistic and formal flexibility have undoubtedly earned him a prominent role at the forefront of our literary culture. To understand Jim Grimsley consequently provides a valuable stepping stone for understanding the ever-evolving state of vital currents of American literature and culture.

CHAPTER 2

The Tote-Crell Narratives

After appearing in a German translation titled *Wintervögel* in 1992, *Winter Birds* was published by Algonquin in 1994, launching Grimsley's career as a novelist in the U.S. market. Although he had achieved considerable success in theatrical circles, his first novel was initially rejected by U.S. publishers as excessively bleak. Algonquin, however, agreed to reconsider *Winter Birds* following its European success and sent the manuscript to Dorothy Allison, who later recalled admiring at an intensely visceral level Grimsley's depictions of a "restless desperation and overwhelming sense of danger all too real."[1] Indeed, Grimsley's novel wrenches open uncomfortable windows into the psychic spaces of rural poverty in the United States, particularly in the South, to depict individuals who survive despite near destitution and who work their way into the middle class, with varying degrees of success, fear, and fierce attachments to those who grew up alongside them. Balancing hope and an often quotidian tragedy, Grimsley frequently emphasizes what Allison has described as the importance of "choosing compassion and love, without compromising what is all too painfully known," traits she associates with "the best writing."[2] Part of Grimsley's refusal to compromise necessarily involves describing pervasive forms of emotional, psychological, and physical violence, which can make his early novels, especially, emotionally difficult to read. Still, as Marielle Rigaud has argued, "in spite, or maybe because of this omnipresence of violence, [Grimsley's] narratives manage to put it at a distance, and thus to go beyond its immediate reality."[3] Grimsley depicts a pervasive violence that his characters and his readers have to acknowledge, not to transcend it but to put it in relation with other elements of life. He achieves this balancing through characterizations of complicated, never idealized relationships and through narrative structures that evoke multifaceted mergers of pleasure and pain, which extend into and beyond the present.

Grimsley begins this project with the Crell family in *Winter Birds,* and he extends his pragmatic optimism by tracing the lives of two families, the Totes and the Crells, in his subsequent novels *My Drowning* (English version 1997) and *Comfort and Joy* (English version 1999). Together, these three novels constitute what some critics have called a "trilogy."[4] While Grimsley has remarked that *Comfort and Joy* is "more of a revisitation than a sequel" to *Winter Birds* and, implicitly, to *My Drowning,* these books nonetheless work together to evoke variations on rural poverty and cycles of mental, physical, and sexual abuse, as well as the relationships within successive generations of one extended family.[5] In doing so, these novels argue that our understanding of individual subjectivities can be shaped and reshaped over time. Their narratives, particularly when considered in conjunction, use this mutable subjectivity to insist on the potential for only qualified escapes from trauma, escapes effected through a fantastical realism, through education, through migration to urban areas, and through an ascendance into the middle class, all of which never completely dissociates individuals from the painful mixture of the abuse and the love experienced in childhood.

Winter Birds

Grimsley quickly imbues *Winter Birds* with depictions of a weathered pastoralism set in eastern North Carolina, an environment fraught with violence through which Danny Crell, his young semiautobiographical protagonist, must move with an almost constant caution. To foreshadow Danny's need for care, the narrative opens amid a casual, uncritical aggression that throughout the novel will threaten seemingly fragile attempts at survival in an inhospitable world. As birds gather castoffs from cornfields, Danny's "brothers lie hidden in the weeds with their shared gun, waiting to burst open bird skulls" while laughing, their BB gun a plaything to be treated carelessly (1). The boys shoot the birds not for food or to protect seeds but for their communal entertainment, their laughter amid the shattered skulls indicating their naïve ignorance of the pain that they have caused. This roughly indifferent violence echoes the domestic abuse occurring in the boys' nearby home, as their father shouts at their mother. The boys are torn between wanting to run from their father and wishing to protect their mother, and their actions signal a reiteration of learned cruelty that inspires them to dominate what little they can of the world around them, if only to assert some form of control over their environment. Grimsley evokes a painful irony as he simultaneously implicitly compares the children to the birds searching for some sustenance in a world that is largely indifferent to their needs and in which they must remain vigilant just to subsist. The boys lying hidden echoes the tense alertness that intensifies throughout the narrative as Danny, his siblings, and their mother repeatedly watch and wait for their father, Bobjay Crell, behind windows and doors and in weedy yards, fearing his returns, his rages, and his fist and feet. This waiting takes place in an anxious solitude as characters both dread the passing of time that brings Bobjay closer and anticipate a time when they can somehow escape from him and from their domestic isolation.

To draw his audience into this waiting, Grimsley uses a subtly layered second-person present-tense narration, which works to implicate readers in the thought processes and the experiences of Danny himself. The novel begins with Grimsley luring readers into an initially nameless, relatively isolated, peace-seeking, and anxious subjectivity that navigates through antagonistic surroundings: "Out past the clapboard house in the weeds by the riverbank your brothers are killing birds" (1). The "you" of this "your" is held here in suspension, separated from home, from family, and from the killing. Grimsley initially withholds a direct referent to this "you," so his narrator might be addressing whoever holds the novel or a young child or both, a technique that works to place Grimsley's reader into this weedy world of still ambiguous violence. Only gradually, four paragraphs later, does Grimsley name the character "Danny," thereby distancing the "you" that could be the reader from a particular boy, perhaps Grimsley's or the narrator's younger self considering his detailed knowledge of events, although this autobiographical element is never explicitly confirmed in the text (2).[6] The persistent second-person mode nonetheless enmeshes readers in Danny's consciousness, as Grimsley invites them to assume Danny's experiences and his fears. This use of the second person likewise blends poignantly a life perceived objectively from the outside or from a distance with the more intimate, differently knowing perspective of someone who has lived it. This intimacy increases in intensity when Grimsley reports that Danny has hemophilia. "Always," the narrator informs the reader, "you watch where you step, checking to make sure there's no glass underfoot, nothing to turn your ankle on, no place to fall" (16). Danny's need to avoid bleeding strengthens the recurrent necessity of escaping the roughness of his father, while Grimsley's description of this need via the present tense and the words "always" and "you" adds an urgent immediacy to it even if readers do not themselves have hemophilia, as the image of a small child bleeding uncontrollably provides an underlying sense of danger and a reminder of the betrayals that any physical body can inflict on the mind within it.

This balancing of referents to the "you" is tricky, and Grimsley deftly resists insisting on associations between his readers and his protagonist. This resistance enables Grimsley to focus on Danny and to shift from an apprehensive waiting to a painful yet positive remembrance of events in Danny's life, an effect achieved by swerving from the present to the past tense. By the novel's third chapter Grimsley's narrator addresses Danny specifically to recall his childhood, now thankfully concluded: "In those days, Danny, you slept in the same room with your brothers and Amy Kay, in the same bed with Allen. . . . The house by the river was always cold, wind pouring in through cracks" (18). The narrative becomes a more personal examination, while its retrospection hints at a future progression in Danny's life, a move from poverty to a middle-class existence where he can sleep in uncrowded rooms and without cold weather invading a dilapidated house. Consequently, if the formalistically unconventional second-person mode in the present tense inspires an anxious immediacy because of Danny's unhappy environment, in the past tense it suggests improvement and emotional relief from that childhood bleakness. Occasionally, Grimsley balances the past and the future, as when he reminds Danny, "after you move out of this house you will live in seven others with your family, before you are old enough to make your home wherever you choose" (18). The narrator intimates that someday Danny will have at least some agency over his surroundings and over his life—but not yet. Intimations of this improved future provide relief for Grimsley's audience and for the narrator if not quite for young Danny himself, who remains in a state of uncertainty, only suspecting or hoping for the more comfortable future in store for him.

This implication of Danny's future agency projects, then, a qualified hope against the present, which exists amid a seemingly unbreakable cycle of economic hardship and abuse. After Bobjay loses his arm in an accident involving a corn harvester, the family moves through several houses, each in various stages of dangerous dilapidation.[7] This domestic architecture echoes the decay in the Crells' domestic peace. Danny and Amy signal the varying reiterations of poverty and violence through their tendency to name the houses they live in, such as the "Snake House," into which snakes slither through its various holes; the "Ice House," which has "one heater" incapable of warming the bedrooms in winter; and, most tellingly, the "Circle House," the design of which allows their mother to "run around" it "forever, and never get caught" (19, 26, 87–88). The image of Ellen Crell running in circles to flee Bobjay evokes the cycles of destruction from which she and her children work to escape not only in this house but throughout their lives, a process Grimsley traces in his subsequent novels *My Drowning* and *Comfort and Joy*.

Escape proves particularly difficult for Ellen because of her tendency to misidentify both her own and others' motivations or emotions, which leads to her falling into old patterns. Describing one flight from Bobjay, the narrator reflects: "Maybe it has come to your Mama now: the knowledge that your Papa and her Daddy are the same man, that maybe the feeling your Papa first gave her was no more than that; maybe something in her made her pick Bobjay Crell because he was like the Daddy she had known all her life, and maybe the feeling never was love" (133–34). Grimsley presents the horrible cycle of abuse in which an attempt to break out only spirals within a circular pattern, where one mistakes for a fresh hope a new angle of an old terror. Equally as awful, perhaps, is the fear that one will perpetually mistake the monster for the lover until it seems too late, while never recognizing the lover at all.

Indeed, Grimsley depicts how confusion over or even a deliberate betrayal of family love can create a recurring perversion of domestic intimacy. At Thanksgiving one year, Bobjay punishes Ellen for an imagined affair by having sex with her visiting sister, leaving a used condom where Ellen can find it. Confusing his love for Ellen with his jealousy over her general desirability and his own desire for her sister, he works to hurt her. When Ellen confronts him, he calls her "the sneakingest bitch" he "ever met," gets exceptionally drunk, hits her with a "sickening noise," "kicks her" with his "heavy boots," and continues to beat her until she crawls under the house "like a dog" (94, 125, 127). These scenes trigger Ellen's memory, which Grimsley subsequently narrates in *My Drowning,* of hiding from her mother, who was trying to beat her, under a house alongside chained dogs. Ellen repeats her past by marrying a man who echoes not only her abusive father but also her abusive mother, whom Ellen had longed to see as a protector. Analogously, just as Ellen's mother failed to protect herself or her family from abuse and became herself an aggressor, Ellen echoes, despite her best efforts and without herself ever becoming abusive, her mother's failure to provide a safe environment for her children. When Danny goes to comfort his mother, Bobjay accuses her of molesting a dog that he has seen crawling under the house to her (131). Confronted with his own infidelity, he dehumanizes Ellen to distract from his own betrayal of family ties and to make himself feel superior, however hypocritically. His strategy nonetheless fails to assuage his guilt, particularly when he finds Danny crawling out from under the house and he realizes that Danny detests him. "You can hide with your Mama under a filthy house, but you don't even want to talk to your Papa," Bobjay complains, compounding his marital insecurities with jealousy over his wife's relationship with her children. To degrade Ellen further and to destabilize her maternal security, he continues to chase her with a knife outside the house and eventually kills Queenie, a pregnant stray dog to which the children have been relatively friendly, telling his wife, "you are a bitch just like this dog" (185). Bobjay's equation of his wife and child with dogs transforms Queenie and her babies into sacrificial animals, a cathartic means for Bobjay to purge his rage at and his enviousness of the closeness between a nurturing mother and her children, a closeness that he feels excludes him despite his being an essential part of the family. The confusion and blurring of emotions, the past and present, and animality and humanity here horrifically distorts any ideal of family love and leads to bloodshed.

Bobjay's cruel sacrifice of the animals, however, works only partially. This savagery calms Bobjay's fury only until Ellen refuses to have sex with him later that evening, and he punishes her by forcing her to commit incest with Danny. Coerced incest functions here, as elsewhere in Grimsley's work, as a grotesque betrayal and distortion of pleasure, trust, intimacy, parenthood, and marriage. Bobjay purposefully disrupts his family's emotional and psychological closeness as this forced sexual encounter perverts the attachment between Ellen and Danny, forcing them from their roles as mother and son into the roles of unwilling sex partners. The inability, moreover, of Bobjay's murder of Queenie to allay completely his rage suggests a dangerous precedent for Danny's brothers, as this violence troublingly echoes the Crell boys shooting the birds in the opening chapter. This forced incest thereby implicitly evokes fears for these boys' future actions. Grimsley does not necessarily suggest that they will force incest on others, but he does raise questions regarding the lengths these boys might go to when the shooting of animals fails to purge their rage and frustration at their world shaped, in part, by their father.

Bobjay harms his family most directly, yet Grimsley also signals several indirect social causes that facilitate this domestic torture. He evokes these extrafamilial contexts by setting his story primarily and ironically during the Thanksgiving holiday, nominally a time to celebrate both grateful families and a grateful nation that survives through communal interactions, even as these latter exchanges offer the Crells little for which to be thankful. Grimsley highlights certain widespread, if not ubiquitous, late twentieth-century rural American socioeconomic problems that trouble the Crells, such as an inability to establish stakes in the land and in the community's social life. The result, he shows, is the pervasive absence of a stable and therefore familiar and potentially sympathetic community. His narrator reports of Danny's first temporary home that the "family that farmed these fields once lived in this house, but they sold the land long ago and the new owner doesn't even remember their name" (18). From one perspective, this change proffers hope that the past need not dominate the present forever and may even pass from immediate memory, as property and society find new caretakers. Yet, from another perspective, it evidences an uncertainty of tenure resulting from a preference, whether right or wrong, for financial benefits over moral responsibilities to remember others' long-term sacrifices and the value of contributions to the community over time.

This absence of a sympathetic community hastens the Crells' descent into substantial poverty. When Bobjay loses his arm while working on Mr. Luther's farm, Luther tells Ellen that Bobjay "couldn't work" for him "anymore with only the one arm" (23). Luther refuses to find Bobjay other work on his land and quickly evicts the Crells from the house that came with Bobjay's job. Luther prioritizes the most profitable method of running his business rather than finding Bobjay a less physically demanding job and giving him time to recuperate. Subsequently, the hypocritically Christian Mrs. Crenshaw rents a foul-smelling house to the Crells and talks "jovially about Holiness revivals," while "holding out her dough-white hand" for Ellen "to count green money onto." When Ellen requests a brief extension for paying the rent so that Bobjay can "pay on the hospital bill for his arm" to avoid getting arrested, further damaging his ability to earn money, "Mrs. Crenshaw, being a woman of firm business principle," forgoes any move toward Christian charity, despite being relatively well off and well fed herself, and "shook her head no" (26). Perhaps having missed any sermons on charity, Mrs. Crenshaw refuses to help the Crells at her own expense, inhibited in part perhaps by her own limited resources. This refusal forces the Crells to move once more to pick up their lives elsewhere. These business practices may be understandable from a myopic perspective, but a general system of low wages for hard work impedes laborers' ability to accumulate savings, which in turn has negative effects on the larger community as families suffer from poverty, hunger, and frustration, conditions that get quickly overlooked or condemned by more affluent and ostensibly Christian individuals as resulting from laziness.

This alienating community does not excuse Bobjay's insecure viciousness, but it certainly exacerbates it. He becomes increasingly jealous of people with more money and better health, whom he perceives as highlighting his difficulties in providing for his family and in satisfying his wife in diverse physical fashions. He suspects, for instance, an affair between Ellen and a temporary landlord who is overweight but who is comparatively wealthy and who has use of both his hands, which allows him to complete more quickly home repairs for Ellen. As a result of his fears of emasculation, Bobjay comes after Ellen with a knife, stopping only when Danny bites his tongue while running from him and begins bleeding. Subsequently, when the unmistakably more successful photographer Frank DeCapra appears unexpectedly at Ellen's door while traveling to take pictures of "rural people" and houses for "a project for [a] university sociological resources center," an indirect extension of Walker Evans and James Agee's work in *Let Us Now Praise Famous Men,* she understandably fears him.[8] This is in part because she knows how Bobjay will respond: "she didn't want Papa to see a man like this one, young, with both his arms intact, dressed in clothes like these and driving a car like that, with that arrogant look in his eyes" (73, 75). Ellen knows that the man's material success, his fine leisurely job, and his bodily wholeness will recall to Bobjay his own deficiencies. Bobjay proves Ellen right, and when he arrives home to find the man leaving he implies that DeCapra took an interest in the Crells' house only to have sex with Ellen. Initially Bobjay gives Ellen not "the look she expected. Not mean. . . . Just scared and hurt"; he subsequently yells at DeCapra, saying, "I'll find you and break your neck" if he uses any pictures of Ellen (86). The overriding atmosphere for Ellen is fear of physical violence, but Grimsley takes the time to relate this scene from Bobjay's perspective, particularly his worry that the photographer's aura of success has caused his wife to betray him, perhaps sexually but certainly emotionally or psychologically. To calm Bobjay, Ellen consistently has to be wary of his suspicions of other men, for which he compensates with hyperaggressive actions, as, shortly after DeCapra's visit, he begins to torment her yet again.

As Ellen's experiences indicate, there are gendered as well as economic forces that shape these alienating networks. Ellen must navigate a community of men who consistently force her into degrading and dangerous positions, who fail to take her fears seriously and even take advantage of them. Bobjay is her chief victimizer and the most difficult to escape, but other men offer her little better. To the unvoiced question of why the Crells fail to leave Bobjay Ellen's inevitable response is, "Where would we go? Where do we have a place?" (90). Who would finance the family and allow them to stay together in a male-dominated rural culture that has given Ellen little chance at economic or professional independence? Grimsley uses DeCapra to evoke the indirect culpability of half-interested economic, intellectual, and often male outsiders. DeCapra is arrogantly and foolishly at ease both in the rural space and with Ellen. He explicitly disrespects the Crells by invading their home and by insulting them, thereby compounding their difficulties. Looking at him, Ellen notices how he "walked across the road as casually as if it were his own kitchen floor"; moments later he has knocked on her door and "pushed past her into the living room," asking, "may I come in?" (72–73). DeCapra asserts, without justification, his educational, social, economic, and gendered privileges by forcing his way into Ellen's house and asking for permission only after he is inside, with no thought for her right to control her home or for her sense of safety.

Once inside, moreover, he treats Ellen as a scarcely important exhibit in a zoo to which he has almost unlimited access. Talking at Ellen rather than with her, "he hardly seemed to notice her; he kept busy browsing the room, the furniture, the plastic curtains at the windows" (74). Despite Bobjay's fears, DeCapra takes little interest in Ellen other than as a dehumanized aesthetic object as he refuses to respect her requests. When she tells him, "my husband will be home soon. He doesn't like me to have strangers in the house, so I'll have to ask you to get all your pictures taken as quick as you can," he flouts her obvious plea by moving slowly and "inspecting the walls" (74). Following Ellen's hint, he even uses what little he can intuit of her life against her with unconscionable disregard for the potential consequences. Overriding her reluctance to let him photograph her, he retorts, "I'll stand right here till your husband comes home. And then he'll be jealous." DeCapra bullies Ellen by capitalizing on his careless perception of her conflicting desires to avoid domestic trouble and to be admired despite her impoverishment. Eventually, her longing to believe that she is pretty enough for someone to want her picture works in conjunction with her anxiety over Bobjay's imminent return (77). Grimsley intimates the consequences of DeCapra's aggressive naiveté when the photographer mistakes Ellen's genuine apprehension for an aesthetic performance when she hears Bobjay's truck. He takes her picture, telling her, "that's the right expression. . . . Pensive. A little worried" (82). Ellen has cause for worry as Bobjay responds to this situation with violence, as discussed earlier, and then by starting to drink again after a brief period of sobriety, leading Ellen to know that their "time of peace had ended" and causing her to become, understandably, afraid (86).

In the midst of such volatility, Grimsley depicts how fantasies can provide a critical escape from violence and anxiety, particularly for children. For mental and emotional self-protection, Danny imagines a being he calls "River Man," a powerful, earthy, superhuman protector, "broad as an oak tree and strong as a bear," who can counter his father's viciousness and his mother's relative powerlessness. In this world of instability, the River Man exhibits a consistent, if evolving, concern for Danny's well-being. When Grimsley first introduces the figure, Danny dreams of the "River Man again," indicating his already recurring role as Danny's caretaker, one who, the narrator reminds Danny, "calls you his son. . . . You see in his eyes every minute how he cares for you" (10). The River Man serves, then, as a useful paternal substitute for Bobjay, with his cruelty to his family, which severely compromises even Danny's mother's guardianship.

If initially Danny sees the River Man as an ideal father figure, this conception quickly collides with his burgeoning sexuality. The River Man comes to function, as Ed Madden suggests in his study of what he calls Grimsley's "gay and gothic gospel," as a "lover/savior" figure, as someone who might comfort Danny and rescue him from his real world, offering him an all-encompassing respite.[9] These themes in *Winter Birds* thus anticipate the more overtly Christian iconography of *Dream Boy,* although the rhetoric in the former eschews Christ-like sacrifices to explore less explicitly spiritual forms of physical pains and pleasures, which an eight-year-old might be on the verge of intuiting without quite understanding. The narrator recalls to Danny how through his dreams, reveries, and memories his relationship with the River Man turned erotic, suggesting Danny's developing reassessment of his longings in relation to male figures. The narrator recollects a "bright lion, loping large-thighed across the grass. . . . The vast paw lifts, a playful tap. . . . You gasp at the tearing . . . you shudder and step away slowly, heart exploding in bursts of heat—the lion eager . . . warm red tongue on your hands" and later the pain in Danny's "leg" (13). Young Danny intuits what he only later understands as the intersecting and fusing pains and pleasures of sexual behavior and romance. Allusions to bounding, bursting, thighs, legs, hearts, and tongues imply erotic and romantic sensations just barely submerged within an awakening, pre-adolescent consciousness. The lion offers a symbol of power, brilliance, a desired object, all of which Danny wants but which he senses will cause him emotional and physical pleasure mixed with pain, the latter coming with a heightened alarm because of his hemophilia. Danny mentally assuages this alarm by blending a primal animalistic force with the more tender, more human River Man, who cares for him after his encounter with the lion by placing him in bed and wishing better for him as, the narrator recounts, he "rises up tall and dark, a warm shadow, . . . sliding beside you" (16). Danny indicates maturing anticipation of his homosexuality as he shifts his erotic longings from the lion to the protective, previously paternal but now more loverlike River Man.

A too extremely intense trauma, however, causes Danny to leave behind the shadow of the fantastical River Man for a bleak yet pragmatically optimistic turn toward objective reality. Grimsley shapes Danny's growing intuition of and confusion regarding the uneasy relationship between pleasure and pain, love and romance, and eroticism and revulsion with a shocking jolt that comes at the height of Bobjay's abuse. Bobjay forces Danny to commit incest with his mother, resulting in the boy's first sexual encounter with another person via Bobjay's indirect rape of his wife and son. Grimsley's narrator reports this event retrospectively, shifting between the day after and the horrific night to represent a fearful anticipation and disruption, which eventually brings clarity. After Bobjay takes Danny from his room at night, for instance, Grimsley inserts a chapter break and picks up the story the next morning. Grimsley thus evidences Danny's attempts to distract himself by focusing on external, after-the-fact details, as when in the morning he ventures away from the house, paying attention only to the frozen landscape in front of him: "When Mama's image tries to reappear you shake your head again. It passes. Only the icy ground remains, and nothing there can harm you" (204). This narrative strategy distances the rape, however slightly, making it less immediate and yet more intense by drawing out the inclusive, second-person account. The narrative structure, this is to say, mimics Danny's cognitive processing, indicating how he both recalls the event, which he cannot help but do, and interrupts his recollections with thoughts of the objective, impersonal world around him, such as the ice or the nearby river. Danny purposefully concentrates on the present environmental coldness, which has a deadening effect on his emotions and accordingly enables difficult insight. For when Danny goes down to the river thinking of his River Man, he realizes that his mother too must have fantasies that contrast starkly with her actual life. He recalls from the previous evening Ellen's "eyes closing," and in the cold clarity of the morning he comprehends that "against her dreamy lids floated the image of her own River Man, and while papa held you against her she dreamed of a world in which you and Papa and all the others had never existed" (208–9). This epiphany causes Danny to abandon his own River Man in favor of more material facts that seem less likely to delude him about his position in the world.

Grimsley fashions this turn toward an objective realism as a step toward maturity and self-improvement. Danny "will return to the river" during his stay in the Circle House, but, rather than the River Man, his focus will be Queenie's grave, which will be a "channel marker" to signal that facts are his "only friends" (209). Fantasies, Danny realizes, if provisionally useful, will fail him as they have failed his mother. Consequently, he turns to a bleak realism that nonetheless offers hope for the possibility of effecting real change. By acknowledging directly the disadvantages of his family's cycle of poverty, lack of education, and abuse, a history that will never quite be overcome, Danny discovers concrete goals toward which to work. Ultimately, as Grimsley indicates in *Comfort and Joy,* this strategy proves successful as Danny goes to college and acquires a middle-class job and a partner who is a problematic but tangible and reliable embodiment of the human qualities of his River Man. These successes are all in the future, but Danny's turn away from fantasy at this moment is a significant advance along the road to an imperfect yet substantial happiness.

My Drowning

Ellen and Danny continued to interest Grimsley, and in 1997 he published *My Drowning,* in which a now elderly Ellen recalls her childhood as part of the Tote family, her young adulthood when she was married to Bobjay Crell, and, briefly, her second, much less tumultuous marriage to Ray Burley. These recollections represent Ellen's attempt to assess and to celebrate, however cautiously, her hard-won independence from poverty and from parental and spousal abuse. Through this attempt, Grimsley goes beyond Ellen's personal story to imagine how two successive generations of women, primarily Ellen and her mother,

Louise, can exist in such drastically different circumstances, with Ellen rising to the myriad comforts of a middle-class life from her mother's abject scarcity. Refusing to romanticize progress, Grimsley uses a nonlinear retrospective narrative that recounts the past amid interspliced scenes from the present to demonstrate the inescapability of memories and a slow, troubled progress. This structure of "constant shifting," as Marielle Rigaud has suggested, "paradoxically blurs the *actuality*" of any given event in Ellen's life "while clarifying it for a final understanding."[10] Consequently, this structure allows Grimsley to argue for the far-reaching influence of memories on the present, so that the past, the present, and the imagined future, while clearly distinguishable, are yet so closely intertwined that even diversely interpreted or misinterpreted recollections, themselves reiterated over time, take on their own reality. This reality, Grimsley shows, simultaneously constrains behavior, emotions, and psychology and offers an impetus to refashion destructive patterns.

My Drowning begins by echoing the oppressive pastoral opening of *Winter Birds,* while more optimistically interrogating the complexities of memory, interpretation, and the potential for reassessing the past through the present. As Danny's story starts in the fields near a river with boys shooting birds, Ellen's starts in her "clean kitchen" as she remembers herself and her sister watching their mother, Louise, slip "beneath the surface of a river" and then observing as she "sobs in the woods" (1, 3). This memory offers greater ambiguity, as it represents a lingering past, with Ellen standing in her kitchen while recalling her childhood, as well as a potential baptism, her mother's possible failed suicide, and even a possible infanticide, for, as Ellen's brother Otis will unreliably report decades later, their mother attempted "to drown" Ellen when their father, Willem, an occasional tenant farmer, beat Louise for bearing yet another child they would have to feed (247). Louise's and Ellen's ultimate survival from the river, however, indicates a renewal or at least a continuation of life and therefore a sense of hope. This is particularly so as Grimsley strategically juxtaposes Ellen's memories of an almost unimaginably underprivileged childhood with her comfortable present in her tidy, well-stocked kitchen. The first-person narration, moreover, provides a greater sense of agency than the more narrowly retrospective, observational second-person narration of *Winter Birds.* It emphasizes Ellen's attempt to shape her own life, with her agency resulting from her determined efforts to escape the irrational horrors of her childhood and to attain some contentment in old age.

While Grimsley starts with an older Ellen, he takes care to show through flashbacks how her rationalized agency developed over time. He presents this process through her gradual understanding of how the irrationality of a community's abuse and ignorance transmuted into the figure of the monster that allegedly terrorized the rural county of her childhood. Ellen's mother and siblings, she remembers, often "feared the monster who lived in the woods around Moss Pond" (18). As opposed to Danny's privately comforting River Man, the monster represents a public legend made manifest from fears of the violence of men, directed primarily at adults and children who cannot bring themselves to articulate or realize fully the source of their trauma. The monster's shadowy existence embodies the anxiety stemming from the uncertainty of knowing when these men might strike, although, unlike the mysterious monster, signs of this violence exist in visible, tangible, concrete forms, such as physical injuries and tears. As Ellen matures, she begins to realize the human nature of the monster. Riding a bus, Louise and her children overhear two African American boys discussing how their mother had seen a "gray thing," the "monster," eating their dog, an interpretation that another African American rider dismisses as originating in their "Daddy's liquor" (101). The woman implies either that the boys' mother had seen their drunk father killing their dog, much as Bobjay does in *Winter Birds,* or that their mother had herself killed the dog in an alcoholic haze caused by their father's liquor. This woman's application of logic to explain the mystery of the monster remains with Ellen. As a middle-aged woman, Ellen uses this logical process to recognize an analogously intimate human conception of the monster. When Willem finally lies dying, Ellen watches with her sisters and observes that he "frightened us, even weak, dying, and hardly able to move," and she connects him through a comparison to "the Moss Pond monster" (250). Notably, intuiting or even recognizing the human source and the mortality of the monster may partially mitigate its ability to create terror, but this ultimately fails to overcome the emotional or psychological damages that are so uncritically entrenched in the Tote children's consciousness.

The monster's staying power persists, in large part, because it draws strength from more than particular individuals and thereby survives even the deaths of its particular human sources. When Ellen revisits Moss Pond later in life, she stops briefly at a store and finds the community once again preparing to hunt the monster. The monster's reappearance and the quasi-ceremonial gathering at the store signal the recurrent, communal nature of the situation. An older resident recognizes Ellen and tells her, "it was always here, the monkster was . . . it was here when you were a little girl, and it was here when your daddy was a little boy. . . . Nothing brings people around here together like that monkster does" (255). The monster represents not only a present, private threat to families but also the haunting communal horrors of the past, which the community fails to recognize for what they are and so fails to eradicate and in effect perpetuates. Ellen recognizes this when she suspects that the monster's most recent reappearance might have stemmed from someone having seen her "through the tangles of branches, searching in the pond for [her] own ghost" (257). The ghosts of the past fuel the monster in the present, which itself will influence the future just as Willem's ghosts, his impoverished and vicious childhood, inevitably influenced Ellen's and as hers will influence her children's in *Winter Birds*. Fear of the monster, moreover, provides a perverse rationale for preserving the very communal structures that are self-destructive. Women stay with men whom their families cannot afford to leave even though these men fail to protect them from almost anything substantive. The false comfort of being together, even in a community that facilitates violence, is easier than acknowledging the destructive elements of society or facing unknown dangers. In a ritualistic gesture, the men in the community hunt the monster, but their ignorance and their refusal to change prevent their killing it and so the ritual fails. Ellen, conversely, like the African American woman who attributes the monster to liquor, has fostered enough objective thought to deduce the human sources of the ghost. Like the African American woman, then, Ellen has taken some steps that provide if not complete freedom from the monster, then at least self-awareness.

Analogous to her relationship to the monster, much of Ellen's evolution to self-awareness arises from her attempt to untangle the mystery surrounding her mother, how her remembered love for Louise could persist despite the latter's unhealthiness, ignorance, indolence, and cruelty (252). In her mind, Ellen sees her mother's "heavy belly, her rolling thighs" dripping with water from the river, looking at her "with the blankness of a cow," and she notes, "I am so in love with her, every part of me aches" (2). Ellen remembers how, because of the exploitative economics of tenant farming, laziness, and a lack of opportunities, her parents failed to provide enough food to feed the family, so that in her childhood Ellen "never ate fast enough to fill [her] stomach" and the "hollow fist in [her] belly" was sometimes attenuated by only "half of a biscuit," while her mother consistently fed Willem and her boys first (3). The Totes' economic destitution far surpassed the Crells' and was compounded by an almost doubly abusive environment, as Ellen's mother often proved as vicious as their father. After fighting one day with Willem, Ellen recalls that her mother reasserted some control in her house: she "kicked me," "struck my face," and "slammed my head" against the wall until "I hid under the house," an anticipation of Ellen's experience in *Winter Birds* (66). Physically, intellectually, and emotionally unable to improve her living conditions, Louise punishes her daughter as an easy way to make herself feel stronger.

The mystery of Ellen's love for her mother grows still more complicated as Louise becomes complicit in Willem's harassment of their daughters. Willem rapes and strikes his eldest daughter, Nora, raising welts, after a boy flirts with her, before turning to Ellen, who starts "listening for something, a step in the night," and starts bathing when she thinks her father is away, only to find him occasionally watching her with a smile (224, 233–34). On a basic level, Willem's transgressions come from his misogynistic treatment of his daughters as his property and his uncontrolled desire for physical pleasure. He also implies hypocritically that his punishment of his daughters for possibly flirting with boys fits into conventions of protecting young girls' chastity, and perhaps he half-believes this proclaimed intention. Exploiting this hypocritical motivation and motivated by jealousy, Louise characterizes Nora as promiscuously parading after a boy and warns that Ellen will soon "be getting boys to send [her] that love mess in a letter" in the hope that Willem's sexual interest might turn into disgust at his daughters' shamelessness, enhancing his desire to beat them rather than molest them (228–29). Through her vengeful moralizing, Louise fuels Willem's physical if not sexual abuse of Nora and Ellen.

Nonetheless, Ellen's personal agency, reinforced by the first-person narration, stems from a desire to find and to echo loving aspects of her mother even as she rejects the violence and poverty that Louise facilitates. Michael Newton has noted that in *My Drowning* "callous acts are expected; it is the moments of generosity that are unforeseen" and that these are the moments that Grimsley celebrates amid the suffering.[11] This is particularly true with regard to Ellen's reflections on Louise. These tensions of expected "callous acts" and unexpected generosity fuel much of the narrative as Ellen sifts through her mother's failures and successes. Ellen's memory of an early Christmas, for instance, evokes largely positive memories of her mother. Ellen recalls her father accusing Louise of shaming him by putting up a Christmas tree one winter. Willem misinterprets Louise's tree as a reminder that he can scarcely afford even the cheapest presents and not much food for his children, but Ellen's older brother Carl explains that the littlest children "never had a tree" (11). Risking Willem's violent reaction, Louise attempts to bring her children some holiday joy, taking a risk that Ellen will emulate for her own children. Ellen also recalls her mother and her sister Nora making some effort to protect her from molestation when they warn her "over and over not to be alone" with Uncle Cope, Willem's brother (5). Louise's protection is inconsistent, but here she joins with Nora to create a tenuous community of women for protection against men. Finally, Ellen recalls the events before she was chased under the house and how her mother, fearing that Willem was about to get arrested for helping Cope to break into a store, whispered to herself that "I won't have anybody," no matter how undependable or belligerent, to help her and her children (70). When she remembers this scene later in life, Ellen too has feared being unable to care for her children because she had so little support, which is largely why she remained in her first marriage, and so she now understands the anger, the anxiety, the helplessness, and perhaps even the maternal urges that sparked her mother's whisper. As young Ellen grows older, goes to school, and discovers how other families live, she considers her mother's body, relationships, and mind, and she revolts, thinking, "I will not live like this." Yet, over time, she can better determine the small acts of kindness amid overwhelming difficulties that inspired her love of Louise and why she herself had to "stand in judgment" of Louise in order to learn what she could from her without repeating her mistakes too consistently in her own life (211).

Ellen's memories of her mother, moreover, allow her to measure gradually, painfully, and yet effectively her own attainment of financial and emotional stability. Fashioning a nonlinear narrative structure, Grimsley slides between recollections to suggest how the past can coexist with and inform the present, revitalizing personal histories in often uncomfortable, if helpful, ways. Grimsley demonstrates this tendency by having Ellen merge realities, past and present, to compare emotions and events with a relatively analogous intensity and thereby to understand her own difficult progress. Late in life, as she increasingly blurs mental barriers, Ellen reflects, "memory becomes as real as the real thing" (2). Ambivalent benefits come from this, as Grimsley depicts in the chapter "In the Present," which begins with Ellen's visceral recollections of completing childhood morning chores such as emptying out the slop bucket with its "tendrils of stink" and "hauling water" for cooking as Nora berated her and Louise "cuffed [her] across the face" for not moving fast enough (184, 186, 188). Interspersed with these memories, an elderly Ellen in her modern kitchen notes that "a rage comes on me . . . strong enough to . . . rob my breath . . . as if one of my brothers or husbands or uncles or my daddy . . . or some other man has asked me to bring him something that he is probably sitting in plain sight of. . . . The voices wait at the ready. I have heard them all my life. . . . The vivid present brings up the vivid past" (186–87). These interlocking passages symbolize structurally how Ellen's emotional and physical responses to past indignities are real and present and will always affect her, if to varying degrees. These powerful involuntary memories of hunger, fear, and degradation, however, add depth to Ellen's appreciation of her subsequent financial and emotional stability. She contemplates her situation: "food cools in the refrigerator, enough to last for weeks. My own little Saturn sits in the yard, in case I need to shop for more. . . . Carefully placed furniture fills every room and carpet warms the floor wherever I want it. All these things belong to me" (202–3). In a conventionally linear narrative structure or if Ellen had tried harder to forget her past, this list of items would be a fairly shallow evocation of a middle-class life. Grimsley's process of contextualization insists on the value of Ellen's acquisitions, her abundant food, her modern amenities, and, most important, her control of herself and her surroundings. If she will never not worry about food or security, the pains of the past evoked by the pleasures of the present give her a greater comprehension of the worth of her successes.

Grimsley's repetition of a river motif throughout *My Drowning* serves as an effective metaphor for this presentation of memory as fusing, fluid, simultaneous, and at times transcendent, especially when conjoined with unknown or scarcely definable details. Ellen's opening vision of Louise in the river, for example, becomes an amalgamation of suicide, a possible murder, and a baptism all at once as memory itself becomes a metaphor for a mental or even spiritual state of being that transcends time, place, and comprehension—an idea that Grimsley explores in more depth in *Dream Boy* and in his science fiction and fantasy novels. In *My Drowning*, memory as a spiritual state of being offers an aching solace. As Nora dies, old and surrounded by her family, she speaks of a "blue-flowered dress," which she and her sisters had loved, fought over, and forgotten in their youth, the significance of which only Ellen can try to explain to Nora's confused children (243). Ellen remembers back through fighting, jealousies, and injuries to a time when she was very young and loved Nora. Ellen reflects, "I understood what memory was for, then. She and I remained there, those little girls lost in the river; we are together even now as I am remembering, and she is dead, and we will be there when I die, forever" (244). This metaphysical riverlike existence, both before and after death, provides a shifting symbol of love conjoined with hate, jealousy, loss, and plentitude across time, as Ellen and Nora's children give each other mitigated access to half-understood details of Nora's life, the combination of which inspires an intuition of an existence beyond death and nothingness.

While Grimsley explores this fluidity of memory in each of his novels, the Tote-Crell trilogy allows him more room to trace the extended resonance of memory over time as events occurring in one novel influence, intensify, and complicate tensions and solaces that erupt in the others. Ellen's echoing memories of hiding under houses from abusive family members provide one example of this process. A second, more positive example grows out of the remembered Christmas scene in *My Drowning*, which comes to resonate with and prepare for the tension of a Christmas time when Ellen is in her fifties. In *Comfort and Joy*, an adult Danny brings his lover, Ford, a wealthy physician, to the comfortable trailer shared by Ellen and her second husband, Ray Burley, for Christmas. Ellen's family's poverty during her early holidays, when she was a child and, later, during her horrific first marriage, contrasts wonderfully with her later ability to celebrate in relative wealth and security. Yet when Ford buys an expensive coat for Ellen, in part a displaced symbol of his love for Danny, his ability to buy such an extravagance on a whim depreciates, however unintentionally, Ellen's family's achievements in a way that Ford cannot understand and that consequently angers Danny. Ellen has come a long way from her mother and from her own childhood, but always, Grimsley reminds us, in a qualified sense, as her memories remain with her. Nonetheless, as Ellen, Ray, Danny, several of his siblings, and Ford all share a Christmas meal together, in a cautious yet satisfying peace, they experience a family fulfillment that overlays and permeates the horrors of past holidays for both Ellen and Danny.

Analogously positive, considering the Tote-Crell novels as a trilogy also illustrates the improving educational and financial success of the family across generations. Louise Tote "can't read" and Willem reads little more than "pornographic books," which he struggles with primarily for cheap erotic titillation, a situation that scarcely allows these parents to be effective or inspiring intellectual role models (226, 227). Even so, Louise insists that her daughters, especially, go to school. She tells Nora, "you ain't quitting" school, although Willem had allowed Carl Jr. to stop attending, and she forces Nora to continue making the trek even when she is embarrassed about going to a white school while living in an impoverished African American area (104). Ellen, moreover, refines her grammar while living temporarily with her Aunt Addis, her father's sister, and Addis's partner, Jenny, as Addis corrects Ellen when she uses "ain't" and praises Ellen's attempts to improve her speech (148). Ellen repeats this process with her own children in *Winter Birds,* correcting her son Grove's "didn't do nothing" to "didn't do anything" and reprimanding Amy for saying "durn," a vulgar slang curse (152, 154–55). Ellen notes that she has had "five smart younguns, and she meant to see [them] all in college one day, all doctors and lawyers in fine big houses" (70). Ellen's efforts to educate her children so that they will have materially easier lives bear fruit, as Danny's brother Allen later runs a bank and Danny, although not a doctor, graduates from college and works as a midlevel administrator at Grady Hospital in Atlanta, where he meets Ford. Before moving in with Ford, Danny lives in a quiet, middle-class apartment by himself, and he can afford plenty of food and occasional travel, the benefits of an intellectual and fiscal success that his grandparents never attained.

The Tote-Crell generations' tolerance for diversity likewise increases throughout the novels as Grimsley links better education to greater acceptance of queer relationships. In addition to their influence in favor of hard work and education, Addis and Jenny also provide positive associations for queer relationships that prepare Ellen for Danny's homosexuality and subsequently for his relationship with Ford, which itself represents an unusually stable romantic partnership for this family. For the Totes, same-sex encounters have generally been a subject for mocking laughter and degradation. A report of Cope being raped in prison provokes giggles and smiles among his family, who find an amusing irony in the lecherous Cope being victimized by a stronger man (73). The Totes also rudely dismiss Jenny, as when Addis's sister refers to the couple's chickens as "Addis's chickens," laying "a slight stress on the word 'Addis's,'" which disregards Jenny's investment in their household (157). Addis's mother, Rose, meanwhile, once spits out to her daughter, "you are a whore. . . . You and that friend of yours, laying up in that room wrapped up in Satan," thereby equating a long-term same-sex romance with profligacy and sin, even as these women support this incapacitated old woman whom they allow to live with them (171). Ellen herself sees little evidence of Satanic influence or divine retribution in Jenny and Addis's relationship. Rather, her stay with the women provides her with a supportive environment, good, hard-earned food, and an example of two adults who, while not publicly affectionate, work and live together in a mutually beneficial, if uneasy, partnership. This childhood experience has long-lasting benefits. When Danny brings Ford to his mother's home for Christmas and discusses their relationship briefly yet intimately with his mother, Ellen's cautiously supportive response must derive to some degree from her early positive memories of Addis and Jenny as the best-functioning couple in her family and from their care for her. The differences among Rose, Louise, and Ellen, then, as mothers, suggest a vast increase in tolerance, understanding, and love.

This tolerance, however, crosses boundaries of race much less neatly or optimistically in the trilogy. Racism and homophobia are intricately interconnected in U.S. history and literature, and in his more recent writing, such as *How I Shed My Skin,* Grimsley has worked to examine these issues in the South and in the United States as a whole, although more sustained depictions of them can be found in the work of writers such as Randall Kenan, L. Lamar Wilson, Lisa C. Moore, and Alexis De Veaux, among others.[12] Even in his earlier novels, however, Grimsley tried to consider certain black southern perspectives with care and sensitivity, working hard to avoid overstepping his authority to speak for the experiences of black communities, and he turned to this topic in subtle yet complex ways across the Tote-Crell novels.[13] In particular, he made a clear effort to depict the everyday racism of white individuals, which most overtly hurts the black community but which also proves self-destructive to white racists and their families. In *My Drowning,* Grimsley portrays the black community of Holberta as a key part of the southern landscape, one that serves as a site for exploitation and for unhappy comparison for the impoverished Tote family. When Louise is about to give birth yet again, she tells Willem that they will have to get "the colored midwife" from "Holberta" because they have not paid the white midwife "for the last two times she come" (74, 82). Louise clearly intends to cheat the "colored midwife," who has little chance of getting compensated for her services. Subsequently, the Totes' poverty forces them to move to Holberta themselves, and both the black and the white communities realize that this is a step down for the family. By trying to salvage their place in the white community, the Totes make their own lives more difficult, walking "twice as long" to their previous grocery store in order to avoid the "black store in Holberta" (100). This general refusal to engage the black community on an equal level dehumanizes the Totes' black neighbors and deprives them of additional income, but it likewise wastes the energy and the time of the Totes themselves.

This self-destructive racism repeats itself in *Winter Birds* and leads, if somewhat more indirectly, to more immediately traumatic results for the Crells. When Ellen's sister visits the Crells and has sex with Bobjay, she has come because she caught her boyfriend "in a shed on top of a black girl from down the road" (96). This interracial sexual betrayal, Grimsley implies, plays a large part in Delia's distress, anger, and insecurity, which she attempts to counter through her brief and disastrous affair with Bobjay. Unfortunately, we get no sense of the black woman's perspective on her encounter with Delia's boyfriend because the story is told by Delia, who presumably seeks to demean rather than to understand her rival. Grimsley gives us enough of a sense of the rural poverty and intolerance within this white community, however, to indicate that whatever this woman's relationship with Delia's boyfriend was, it would have been problematic. Delia's own myopia, meanwhile, and her need to reestablish her self-esteem in any way possible destroy her relationship with her sister and help to throw the Crell household into a violent turmoil that leads to Bobjay's sexual abuse of Ellen and Danny. While this abuse does not stem directly from racism, Grimsley carefully constructs this narrative to suggest how white prejudices subtly intersect with and inflame other instances of insecurities, aggression, and abuse, even within white communities.

Grimsley also, however, gives a sense of the knowledge and the physical laboring of black communities, which Ellen and her own children come to respect. In addition to the Holberta woman who realizes that the local "monster" stems, at least in part, from alcoholism, Cunning Bates, a young black boy, tells the Tote children in *My Drowning* about the witch that was hung in a tree behind their house, which heightens the dangerous unfamiliarity of their new living space, a space of which the African American children have a better working knowledge (101). The Totes experience more pragmatic problems in winter when they have to compete in searching for firewood with the local black community, which "knew the country better" (125). Ellen learns, moreover, that race is not a stable indicator of rationality or resourcefulness, as she realizes that the "black women in Holberta made gardens for tomatoes" when her "mama didn't," evidencing the black women's superior food management and work ethic (95). This understanding opens Ellen to reevaluating her approach to the black community, however slightly, and when a well-meaning, if undereducated, friend informs her that she "should not say nigger" but "nigra" in order to be polite, Ellen realizes, to a degree, the importance of this semantic distinction (213). Subsequently, Ellen reports, she spoke "only of 'nigras,' until my daughter taught me to call them 'black.'" Ellen notes that she "made these changes in order to be considered a better quality of person than my own family," which "continued to call black people niggers" (213–14). Ellen reports wanting to be polite and to be considered a better person. In his memoir, *How I Shed My Skin,* Grimsley emphasizes that his white community's semantic concerns over references to race frequently "had little to do with ideas of equality" or tolerance and "everything to do with standards of politeness" and social betterment.[14] Nonetheless, in *My Drowning* Grimsley shapes Ellen's character more sympathetically, again however slightly, regarding racial tolerance, and this emphasis on social niceties signals her attempts to see the value in racial others as integral to her own project of self-improvement.

Indeed, Grimsley reinforces Ellen's attempts to engage African Americans more justly in *Winter Birds.* In one instance, when Danny goes to the hospital as a child, he shares his room with "a little black boy" whose "Mama couldn't always stay with him to comfort him" at night (56, 58). On these nights, Ellen would "stroke his forehead, telling him, 'It's all right, boy. Your Mama loves you and she's coming back tomorrow . . . nobody's going to hurt you while we're here'" until he calms down (58). Acting as it would be difficult to imagine Louise acting, Ellen tells the boy what she would want her own son to hear. Racial differences may not disappear, and several instances of goodwill hardly mean the defeat of social slights, much less systematic and institutionalized inequalities, as Grimsley acknowledges in his memoir. But these differences fade, albeit all too slightly, when faced with the mothers' and the boys' common humanity, and this is a success worth documenting if certainly not overidealizing.

Even though these moments are not extensively effective in addressing racial disparities, Ellen's reconsiderations of race serve as an important facet of her evolution, as does her modeling of racial tolerance to her children. As we have seen, Ellen willingly changes her terms when her daughter corrects her well-intentioned but nonetheless offensive use of "nigra," and Dan echoes the examples his mother set in his childhood when in *Comfort and Joy* he takes interest in the "dreadlocks and yarn hat" of a black cab driver and when he and Ford subsequently agree that they liked the cab driver's hair (1, 4). Dan's casual observations follow his mother's lead, and, if they potentially patronize a seemingly exotic "other," they also signify a substantial distance from his extended family's previous desires to cheat and demean black individuals, such as the Holberta midwife. This scene with the black cab driver, moreover, at the beginning of a novel about overcoming alienated queer experiences, implicitly raises comparisons and potential interconnections among race, sexuality, and socioeconomic class. Grimsley raises but never quite explores these potential interconnections. Consequently, Dan and Ford's brief attention to the driver evokes the absence of what might have been worthwhile investigations into the lives of queer black workers and professionals. This would have been a useful opportunity to trace Ellen's youthful perceptions of the black community in Holberta through to her influence over her son's interaction with the greater racial and socioeconomic diversity of Atlanta and would have provided more of a completeness to *Comfort and Joy* as well as a chance to extend aesthetic resonances throughout the novels in the trilogy.

With superb skill, however, in *My Drowning,* Grimsley deemphasizes Ellen's relationship to her children, male and female, and to men in general in order to explore in greater depth her relationship with the older women in her life. Aside from male family members, Ellen scarcely notes men's names, and this is a formal and an aesthetic strategy that highlights the educational and supportive influences, alongside the degradation and the antagonism, that she seeks in memories of other women, such as her sisters, her mother, her grandmother, Addis, and Jenny. Grimsley uses this strategy to distract from Ellen's socially dominant roles of mother and wife, which he explores in *Winter Birds* and *Comfort and Joy* but which never overwhelm her personal subjectivity. As a result, Grimsley can focus on the early relationships that shaped Ellen's steps toward an incomplete yet solacing independence of body, mind, and spirit. The novel begins and ends with references to Ellen's present-day, well-stocked, personally organized home, where she lives alone after decades of catering to others (258). The intense formal interpenetration of the past and the present, memories weaving and reweaving throughout the novel and bleeding into the present, prevents this symmetry from offering an unmitigated happiness. Yet by ending the novel with a reference to Ellen's present satisfying life, Grimsley reminds us that this image, too, should permeate our engagement with the past narrative, just as it does Ellen's own idea of herself. Grimsley leaves us, then, with the uncomfortable consolation of a woman cognizant of how her hard work, endurance, and mental, emotional, and psychological fortitude have finally gained her some form, however compromised, of a private peace largely influenced by the women in her life.

Comfort and Joy

While *My Drowning* delves into the childhood and the old age of Ellen, *Comfort and Joy* depicts Dan Crell's life after he has left home, graduated from college, established a middle-class life in Atlanta, Georgia, and begun a relationship with Ford McKinney. Although Grimsley has called *Comfort and Joy* weaker than his other work because of its "more romantic" elements, his subsequent reference to the novel's "emotional richness" seems a more apt assessment because it accounts for his convincing depiction of the everyday details of a long-term relationship, one that Grimsley develops through a complex narrative structure.[15] To achieve this, Grimsley traces two interwoven story lines: in the present, Ford's and Dan's introduction to each other's families during the Christmas season and, in the past, their journey to the point where they would want to make such introductions, including the narrative markers of the Christmas season when they first meet and the first one when they are in a relationship. Grimsley uses this interlocking structure to examine Dan's and Ford's struggles to allow themselves to fall in love and to overcome their insecurities in order to have the relationship that they eventually enjoy. While not as overtly structurally experimental as Grimsley's earlier novels, his later science-fiction-fantasy novels, or his drama, *Comfort and Joy* is equally as complex as Grimsley skillfully navigates Dan's and Ford's communal and individual present lives together and their unique pasts and families. If this is Grimsley's most optimistic and sentimental novel, in it he refuses to shy away from the difficulties of maintaining and enjoying a long-term romantic partnership, particularly an unconventional one between men with such different socioeconomic statuses, educational levels, and comfort levels with their sexuality and their families. In the end, however, Grimsley shows Dan and Ford using the liberal tolerance of Atlanta in the 1990s to establish conjointly a private and a public relationship.

Grimsley quickly establishes that Dan has found a tenuous stability with Ford even as the uncertainty still inherent in their two-year relationship makes Dan long for a space to cover protectively the intimacy that they have gained. Grimsley achieves this by beginning the novel with a journey that joins the two men. In the opening chapter, Dan rides in a cab to the airport where he will meet Ford so that they can travel together to rural North Carolina to introduce Ford to Dan's mother and siblings over the Christmas holiday. Christmas in the novel contextualizes the men's fragile attachment; it evokes domesticity and spiritual communities and yet is also a reminder of how certain versions of Christianity can make family relationships difficult for nonheteronormative individuals. As Dan leaves the upper-middle-class house he shares with Ford near the heart of Atlanta, he imagines retreating to it in order to "find a hiding place" (1). Houses, as we have seen, are key emotional and psychological spaces in the Tote-Crell novels, and in Grimsley's more urban fiction architecture more generally offers key thematic insights by linking public and private concerns. Dan and Ford's particular house sets the tone for the retrospective progression of *Comfort and Joy* as, amid flashbacks depicting their difficult coming together, Dan and Ford learn to feel comfortable with each other in private, the house providing a "hiding place" within the busy city and a respite from their respective families. This initial evocation of the shared house, moreover, serves to link *Comfort and Joy* immediately to the rest of the trilogy through Dan's presence in it, and it also introduces Ford, who has managed to purchase the house thanks to his family's substantial inherited wealth and his own financial security from his work as a pediatrician at Atlanta's Grady Hospital.

For Ford, the house represents a space both traditional and new, one that retains traces of his family without its immediate patriarchal constraints and one that allows him to refashion his own life without entirely rejecting his past. Its rooms contain some furniture from Ford's "grandmother" and "from an aunt's house" and some purchased by his mother, yet it also exists away from his parents' conventionally heteronormative upper-class Savannah home with its myriad "family pictures, some dating back as far as the birth of the photograph," which remind Ford of the expectation that he will marry a woman and have heirs (113, 85). When he first invites Dan over on New Year's Eve, a night pointedly symbolic of new beginnings, Ford entertains visions of a long-term relationship different from his family's expectations for him and also different from his previous, primarily physical or emotionally unsustainable interactions with men. Upon returning from the bathroom late at night, Ford thinks, "not only had he made love to Dan Crell but now they rested together in Ford's bed," a train of thought that leads him to reflect, "someone with a heartbeat, waiting" for him (116). Dan is asleep, so the waiting Ford senses may be Dan's unconscious desire for Ford to return to bed that night, but it also signals enduring patterns of Dan staying with Ford and anticipating his return, as well as a more abstract sense of waiting for both men to mature to the degree that they can live together in an increasingly happy and healthy relationship.

Grimsley sympathetically links Ford's hopeful visions of a continued emotional and physical relationship with Dan to Dan's desire to perceive their relationship as the realistic actualization of his childhood fantasies of care and romance. Grimsley does this structurally by shifting subtly yet quickly from the couple's first New Year's Eve together to a scene almost two years later when Dan takes Ford to the Circle House just before bringing him to Ellen's for Christmas. This moment heightens the differences between Dan and Ford, as Dan realizes that the visit to the Circle House scared Ford, who has not previously realized quite how poor the Crells once were (153). More important, it signals how far Dan has committed emotionally to Ford between that New Year's Eve and the present Christmas. In this house, Dan shares with Ford his fantasy of the River Man, which had provided a mental escape from his family. At moments of emotional intensity in Grimsley's writing, as previously noted, the past, present, and future tend to blur, and this happens here as Dan's privately imagined past, signaled by italicized type, mixes with his and Ford's shared present, signaled by nonitalicized type. In the room where Bobjay forced Dan against his mother, Dan remembers, "*I used to lie . . . and dream of a cave beneath the river, a man like you in the cave,*" as Ford's "arm circled Dan from behind." Generally, Dan shares little of his past with Ford, if only to keep them as close socioeconomically as possible to avoid causing tension, but here Dan tells Ford, "I used to dream about you at the river. . . . You lived under the water, and you took care of me. . . . I didn't know it was you at the time. But it was" (123). Grimsley's use of the past tense in the unspoken italicized clauses presents a stylistic distance from the second-person present tense of *Winter Birds* and consequently signals Dan's attempt to put the past behind him, although his return to the house is evidence of the difficulty he faces in doing so. Yet Dan's willingness in this instance to recall his painful past also evokes an optimistic hope. Grimsley's shift between scenes in the two houses as Dan and Ford travel from Georgia through North Carolina cautiously sharing memories thus indicates thematically and formally their reciprocal desire to achieve an honest long-lasting intimacy and to establish connections with each other even when their differences seem most overwhelming.

Grimsley is never so sentimental as to insist on this adult intimacy as dreamlike or to overromanticize Dan and Ford's trajectory, which he filters through a heavy dose of realism. Indeed, he allows Dan to heed his precocious eight-year-old self's realization in *Winter Birds* that facts are his "only friends" and to follow through on this early turn toward pragmatism (209). In *Comfort and Joy* Dan seeks a partner not in an idealized fantasy but in a flawed actual man, and he lives with him in a human-made house surrounded, somewhat like the River Man's cave, with verdant natural protection, set off from public bigotries by "interlaced limbs of cedar," magnolia, and "a deep green veil" (1).[16] As this description suggests, Dan has largely achieved the surreal dreams of his childhood but in practical terms. The references in the opening chapter to natural refuges and to Dan's recollections of the River Man serve as consistent reminders of the passionate if at times tenuous or forgotten dreamlike qualities of what Dan and Ford do achieve, although the novel offers these reminders in the midst of capturing beautifully, as Gary Richards aptly remarks, the commonplace "details of the day-to-day existence of a contemporary gay couple" in the 1990s, such as dealing with pets, finances, careers, and individual desires.[17] The couple's difficulties are in sustaining and navigating an adult relationship in which the men need not hide but can find both comfort and joy living together and interacting honestly with family, friends, and colleagues, a relationship that blends erotic and romantic excitements with the mundane struggles of bills and satisfying often conflicting individual needs.

One of Ford and Dan's primary conflicts in both their public and their private lives stems from Ford's struggle to overcome his psychological discomfort with his homosexuality. While Dan has long acknowledged his homosexuality publicly, even to his family, Ford has remained more secretive, telling only his sister about his interest in men and only directly before he decides to date Dan. In their early months, Ford remains shy and reluctant to identify as gay or to go to queer spaces, such as the "gay bars" in New Orleans when they vacation there (194). Still, Grimsley traces Ford's increasing comfort with Dan as Ford sheds his fear and semiconscious sense of shame during their public interactions. Ford slowly introduces Dan to his friends, and he meets Dan's friends. While traveling to North Carolina, he nervously rubs Dan's sweater on a plane, causing Dan to think, "rarely did Ford touch him so freely in public," and although Dan subsequently observes that "even after two years" Ford seems sometimes unwilling to kiss even in private, he kisses Dan during their first night in a hotel as they travel to Dan's mother's house (10, 13). Each of these scenes evidences Ford's accumulative attempts to be more overtly affectionate and relaxed with Dan, even as Dan must stem his hurt and resentment at Ford's occasional reluctance to acknowledge their mutual desire.

To be fully comfortable together, Grimsley suggests, Dan and Ford have to develop new understandings of queer relationships and kinships and to form new norms. Prior to their second Christmas together, when they are each imagining the difficulties in bringing the other to their respective relatives' celebrations, they both feel alienated simultaneously from their childhood families and from each other. Struggling to find some stability, Ford tentatively articulates their relationship: "We're a family, Dan. You and me. Aren't we?" (274). This combined statement and question indicates an anxious ambiguity, but Grimsley bolsters this new formulation of a family by having already narrated a scene that is still chronologically in the future, as he has described Dan's relatives, including Ford, sitting around a table at Christmas as Dan's sister Amy insists "we're all family" (173). Ellen, too, has anticipated Ford's uncertain perspective by helping Dan to wrap a ring he had bought for Ford as a Christmas present, which Ellen recognizes explicitly as a "wedding ring," her help signaling her blessing (141). Grimsley's nonlinear narrative structure enables him to engage

Ford's doubtful insistence more poignantly and with less anxiety because, structurally, Ford echoes Amy's and Ellen's already narrated assertion that they will embrace Ford as family. Reading of Ford's welcome at Dan's mother's house and the assertion that they are part of a "family," even if not quite as a married couple, helps to mitigate our uncertainty over how to characterize the couple's relationship, even as Ford and Dan's reception helps to normalize their relationship and to modify it to include extended family. Ford's acceptance by the Crells does not create or cement his partnership with Dan, but it certainly consolidates Dan's and Ford's sense of its legitimacy and durability.

While Ford's acceptance into Dan's family fortifies their connections, Ford's process of accepting his same-sex desires really begins in Atlanta amid the opportunities available within this late twentieth-century city. On Ford's first date with Dan, they drive over "the highway monuments of downtown Atlanta . . . bridges, loops and rivers of prestressed concrete, dressed steel beams, and arcs and torrents of masonry" (98). This description of Atlanta's highway interchanges provides a beautifully modern metaphor for the myriad opportunities and the firmly rooted varieties of diverse people, experiences, and tolerances that Atlanta will offer these men, experienced sometimes at a euphorically fast pace and sometimes as slowly as Atlanta traffic inches along during rush hour. Shortly after Ford cancels his first date with Dan out of fear, almost two years prior to their Christmas with the Crells, for example, Ford's mentor at Grady, Dr. Milliken, insists on pausing to hear Dan sing at the hospital's Christmas concert because of his "wonderful voice" (61). Dan's homosexuality is public knowledge at work, so Ford is surprised when an authority whom he respects openly admires Dan. At Grady Hospital Ford also encounters Dorothy Ballard, another medical student, who before she knows that Ford is gay tells him about her Christmas in Atlanta with her lover, which made for "the best holiday" she could "remember in years" (92). Ford both envies and fears Ballard's casual openness regarding same-sex relationships, which can take place more easily in this "crass big city," which Ford considers his new home (89–90). This environment very slowly makes clear to Ford the potential for queer men and women to be honest and open, even with work friends, and to experience minimal rejection or ostracism.

As such, Atlanta facilitates Ford's slowly increasing openness, which itself leads to a normalization of his life that benefits him and Dan, both personally and professionally. When Ford asks Russell Cohen, another physician, to help move Dan into his home, Russell notes the unusualness of the situation, but he treats it relatively nonchalantly. When Ford mentions directly after the move that he looks forward to rotating back to Grady, Russell responds that if his "girlfriend worked at Grady" he "might get to see her now and then." Making this reference to Dan and Ford's relationship, Russell presents it "casually, without any forethought, as if the parallels, in his mind, were exact" (228). Even this casual recognition makes Ford uneasy, but he ultimately appreciates it. As a result of the couple's growing willingness to acknowledge their relationship publicly, their lives become richer in many respects. They have parties for mutual friends, Ellen talks to Ford when she calls Dan, and as "their relationship became common knowledge" at the hospital Dr. Milliken even asks "Ford to use his influence with Dan" to get medical equipment for their unit as "if the request should seem perfectly ordinary" (271). This event tellingly reinforces the significance of Ford and Dan's first meeting at the hospital, when Dan helped Ford with beds for pediatric patients. Through these urban interactions, Grimsley carefully evokes the naturalness of Ford and Dan's relationship, which in turn benefits their friends and even their hospital colleagues, who can work more efficiently, achieving better care for themselves and their patients, by recognizing their relationship. Society, Grimsley demonstrates, is better off if Ford and Dan's relationship is accepted as part of a daily routine.

Grimsley nonetheless acknowledges a lingering homophobia, even in Atlanta. While he elides any physical violence, he signals how intolerance can tarnish his characters' professional and domestic encounters. Before Ford's relationship with Dan becomes widely known, Dr. Harknight at Grady tells Ford to "watch out" for Dan because "he's gay." When Harknight walks off, Ford simply stares "resentfully at the back" of his colleague's head, not yet ready to defend homosexuality publicly or to challenge the other physician's benighted prejudice (109). Even Ford and Dan's house is not completely secure from insult. When Ford finally tells his parents in Savannah about his relationship with Dan, they call Dan at home and accuse him of turning Ford gay, and Dan reports that they threatened to have him fired from his job (262). The house, after all, is not a fantastical river cave but a mixture of Ford and Dan, Savannah and Atlanta, past, present, and future, and consequently vulnerable to bigoted invasive prejudices.

Yet Grimsley subtly insists that sexuality joins religion, class, and gender—if not quite race, as discussed earlier—as conceptions that are becoming less divisive, if far from irrelevant. When Ford's mother calls and refuses to understand why Ford has asked Dan to live with him and Ford refuses to be explicit, Russell Cohen sympathizes by recounting that his "parents hate" his girlfriend, almost certainly because they want their son to marry a Jewish rather than a Christian woman. "You can't let it get to you," Russell advises, although this is easier said than done (233). Still, even seemingly closed circles in Savannah become permeable. Ford's sister Courtenay brings her husband, Mike, a carpenter, to her parents' house despite their oblique insults regarding his social class

(252). With a myopically long memory, Ford's father suggests that Savannah society is no longer the "closed circle" that it was in the "Reconstruction" era, but whether he approves of this change or not remains ambiguous (84). When Ford asks his father if he thinks "it's better now," he responds, "depends on what you mean by better" (85). Ford's parents exult in their advantageous past and their privileged traditions, and they see any change that threatens their ease, position, and affluence as hardly better for their family. Grimsley presents this with some understanding, despite the elitism and rigid definitions of family involved, as Ford's parents only want what they think is best for their children: "There's so much happiness in raising a family, Ford," his mother tells him, "in continuing the family that you're part of" (86–87). Courtenay's cross-class relationship allows her to satisfy the majority of her parents' expectations, so they tolerate it, albeit begrudgingly. The crisis faced by Ford McKinney's parents is that they are willing to sacrifice their relationship with their son should he deviate too far from their wishes as he reinterprets their traditions and definitions of kinship. They fail to realize, Grimsley implies, that Ford could have most of the happiness they want for him and preserve most of their traditions despite being gay, if people such as themselves did not make it so difficult.

Ford McKinney's parents, however, are not the only interpreters of tradition. Ford's Grandmother Strachn advocates, if all too cautiously, for the need to learn from past mistakes in order to redefine sexual and gendered stereotypes. Ford never specifies to his grandmother his reasons for not wanting to marry, but she understands the significance of his situation. In doing so, she draws an implicit, if not quite apt, comparison between her mistake in marrying Ford's grandfather and Ford's situation: "If you don't want to get married, you shouldn't do it. If I had it to do over again, I wouldn't get married. Not to your grandfather" (260–61). Despite being a guardian of Ford's family's rituals and wealth—she herself owns a "well-kept mansion" on "the corner off Calhoun Square" in Savannah—she argues for revising conventional roles pertaining to sex and gender, even if she refrains from discussing these issues in detail (66). Still, to reaffirm Ford's place in his family despite his parents' anger with him, she states overtly that she will not disinherit him: "Your mother is afraid I won't leave you this house if you're single when I die. You tell her I said that's nonsense" (261). Sexuality and marriage, Strachn asserts, will have little influence on her practical and legal will to sustain and to enhance, so far as she can, Ford's affluence and social status. Grimsley does not present Strachn as a powerfully liberal feminist or a supporter of queer rights—she never mentions Courtenay's inheriting houses or Ford's homosexuality—but she represents an interesting case study of analogies between feminist and queer individualists and how a conservative desire to keep a patriarchal inheritance intact can function in an unintentionally liberal-ish fashion.

While Ford's finances and social position remain largely stable despite his sexuality, Grimsley portrays how these unusual benefits can cause discord in a relationship that already must contend with the effort to achieve the right mixture of mutual support and independence. Ford's family has "trust funds" that ensure their comfort, while the closest equivalent that Dan's family has is a "Brunswick stew recipe" that Bobjay's mother "handed to Ellen . . . almost as a trust," a near analogy that echoes briefly but clearly to indicate the financial gulf between Ford and Dan (45, 171). This gulf creates stress as Dan, in particular, struggles to maintain his sense of self-worth and self-confidence while living with Ford. Before meeting Ford, Dan had overcome the obstacles of poverty and abuse by obtaining a respectable clerical job and maintaining an apartment of his own, ensuring a safety and a stability that he had never known while he was growing up. Relinquishing some of this independence to move in with Ford involves accepting a greater vulnerability and a greater sacrifice than Ford can understand. To ensure that he will feel comfortable in a luxurious house that has Ford's name on "the deed," Dan insists on paying rent so that he can feel at home (236). Ford fears that this will make Dan his roommate when he wants Dan "to be something else," namely his lover, although even well into their relationship Ford can barely think this word to himself (239, 240). Ford, moreover, refuses to adjust his expenditures to better fit Dan's income, and Dan frequently rejects Ford's offers to pay for him in order to maintain his relative self-sufficiency and his peace of mind. In general, the men avoid talking about money, which allows lingering resentments to fester beneath a sometimes misleading sense of peace. How to even talk about finances to ensure that each man's needs are met becomes a constant source of tension in navigating their emotional and psychological life together.

An almost equal source of tension stems from Dan's complicated medical conditions and Dan's and Ford's similar coping strategies of alternating between a cautious honesty and silence. On their first date, Dan tells Ford that he has hemophilia and that he is HIV-positive, restraining himself with a "terrible self-control" (105). Ford refuses to let either of them use this as a means to escape intimacy, reminding them both, "I'm a doctor. I know I can't die from being near you. I can't catch this virus from lying in bed next to you, or touching you, and I probably won't even catch it if I do more than just touch you" (107). Still, even the small risk to Ford adds another difficulty to their relationship, particularly through their need to be especially careful during sex. This carefulness carries emotional and psychological implications. They had "safe sex," Grimsley reports, "because they agreed that it was so. Yet it never quite felt safe. So they closed their eyes to any danger, and never, or rarely, spoke about it" (202). As in any relationship, even the strongest, a mixture of honesty and omissions exists as the men deal on their own terms with the dangers entailed by HIV, especially. Dan fears that Ford will consider his blood filthy and leave him, and Ford gets angry at and scared by Dan's cultivated coldness, intended to protect Dan's own emotional stability, his refusal to get too close to a man who might leave him (242, 245). To downplay these anxieties the men generally avoid analyzing them, which leads to a lack of communication that intensifies the uneasiness of their connection.

Dan's hemophilia presents an added anxiety, although Grimsley depicts this as ultimately bringing the couple closer together. As an adult, Dan has largely coped with his bleeding on his own. Ford insists on helping, and this gradually enables Dan to admit his vulnerability in a way that makes the men more mutually supportive partners. Early in their relationship, Ford stops by Dan's apartment and finds Dan trying unsuccessfully to inject himself with his medicine after having bled for quite a while. Frustrated with this self-destructive manifestation of Dan's self-reliance, when "all [he] had to do was make one telephone call," Ford nonetheless moderates his anger at Dan for refusing his help. He takes Dan home and nurses him with a gruff tenderness that "eased something deep" in Dan, "beyond the reach of pain or painkiller" (209). Although these two men will repeatedly clash over this behavior, these eruptions force them to a breaking point where they must reassert their unwillingness to quit their relationship, and so they renew their commitment to each other, having realized that they do not really want to live apart, spend holidays apart, or allow their fears and differences to overcome the comforts and joys of being together (245).

These unique complications are all real and pressing, but so is the broader underlying question of how these men can conceive of long-term queer relationships, particularly relatively equal partnerships between individuals from such different backgrounds, without pervasive and influential social models and reaffirming cultural expectations. Where, Grimsley asks, "is the sense of permanence, where is the tie that binds" two men together? Indeed, one of Grimsley's primary concerns throughout the novel is to explore how and why a same-sex or even, extrapolating a little, any conspicuously unconventional relationship can stay strong with so little social support: no formal marriage; often no children and the kinship ties that they bring; fear of showing affection in public; the assumptions among other people that same-sex couples are simply friends; religious and institutional intolerances. The answer, Grimsley suggests, is the creation and reiteration of new ways of conceiving of families, as he shows Ford and Dan doing, and of committing to intimacy. Grimsley illustrates this latter by describing Ford and Dan's daily life together: "they dreamed in tandem and shared fragments of each other's dreams, and they grew more like each other day by day, not in personality but in the fissures of the brain, because, seeing the same things every day, day after day, they laid down crevices in themselves that were the same shape, that were the same events written into memory, and this was enough, without words, to keep them silent about the fact of their hates and their fears" (207–8). This description of Dan and Ford's life together is troublingly uncertain yet ultimately optimistic. Fears, doubts, and hates will never entirely dissipate, but committing to each other and sharing each other's lives allow them to grow together emotionally, psychologically, and even physically, as joint habits get embodied in their brains.

The final scenes of the novel recontextualize the strain of this process by emphasizing the need for Ford's parents to acknowledge, willingly or not, their son's relationship with Dan. Strengthened by their for the most part welcoming Christmas with Dan's family, the men make an uninvited visit to Ford McKinney's parents' house, itself symbolic of Savannah's high society and its intolerances. Although Dan thinks of the house as forbidding, its once seemingly impermeable boundaries are noticeably crumbling, a process long prepared for by its having once sheltered Courtney's and Ford's adolescent fantasies (283). When the men arrive, the house already contains, albeit only for Christmas, Courtenay's carpenter husband, Mike, whom her parents thought was not the "right kind of boy" for her (87). Ford's arrival with Dan adds an additional social incursion into a conservative stronghold by openly forcing the humanity of same-sex sexuality to the fore of the family's concerns. Before entering the house, Ford had "worried the ring on his finger," Dan's recent Christmas present to him, and "studied it" before deciding to keep it on, even after Dan has suggested that he take it off if its absence would make the encounter with his parents easier (283). While Ford refers to Dan only as his friend in front of his parents, these preparatory actions establish Ford's considered and fully intentional decision to insist on their intimate relationship (287). When pressed, as his parents order Dan to leave, Ford insists on the strength of their intimacy, telling his parents, "if you want anything to do with me you'd better learn to live with him. Because if you want me to choose between him and you, I'm choosing right now. I'm leaving with Dan" (288). Ford makes it abundantly clear that Dan is his partner, part of his family, and that his parents reinforce painful, outdated conceptions of kinship by ostracizing him. Ford openly critiques his parents' conservatism by noting that Dan's family had given Ford himself "a chance" and by informing his parents that "you don't have to make it like this," an interpretation bolstered by Courtenay's verbal willingness to welcome Dan (289). Ford and Dan realize that the elder McKinneys will likely not approve any time soon of their relationship, but in order to move forward successfully themselves, they need to be as forthright as they can with Ford's parents and to offer at least the possibility of a future reconciliation.

Dan's family, Courtenay and Mike, and, more distantly, the couple's Atlanta environment indicate that a reconciliation with Ford's parents may be possible, as they all are evidence that a family's values and beliefs can be flexible, supportive, and evolving. Ford emphasizes how an inflexible conception causes domestic pain, and Grimsley implicitly indicates how the McKinneys' intolerance paradoxically, even perversely, threatens many of the very traditions that they seek to preserve. Ford will never have the life that his parents wanted for him. But if they accept him and Dan, they might still spend holidays with Ford, bequeath their inherited wealth to him, and sustain their social positions as much as possible by not ostracizing him and his partner.

Like many of Grimsley's novels, *Comfort and Joy* ends with bittersweet optimism. While forced out of the McKinneys' Savannah home, Ford and Dan have decided decisively to stay together. They have cemented this commitment before their families and their friends, not with a ceremony, as with conventional marriages, but with a series of events that are differently yet analogously binding, even without religious and legal documentation. They have, significantly, left the door open for Ford's parents to change their minds. Ford tells his parents that he and Dan will spend the night at the McKinneys' beach house on Tybee Island, and his last words to them are "if you change your minds, call us" (289). It seems unlikely that Ford's parents will change their minds quickly, but the two men have each other, good jobs, and their relatively good health. On the island, they walk on the beach with the "bond between them" seeming "so clearly visible that acting it out hardly mattered anymore" (290). Thus the novel begins with both men longing "to find a hiding place" as they leave their Atlanta home and ends with their travels almost complete as they walk together in public (1). Grimsley repeats here his opening line, "*to find a hiding place,*" but its urgency has lessened: although the novel's first and last chapters are set days apart, in the middle chapters Grimsley has detailed how in the past two years the two men have found less a "hiding place" than a "shelter in each other." The novel concludes tenderly as they walk side by side in public before entering a house together (291). Grimsley concludes optimistically with the word "together," a final prediction that the men will stay a couple. Surely they will fight and disagree, but for the most part they will maintain a nurturing, loving, and long-lasting partnership. Finally, while Grimsley leaves us with the two men alone, they do spend the night in the McKinneys' beach house, perhaps hinting that their exclusion from Ford's family is only temporary. Regardless, ahead of them is their fortunate, welcoming life back in Atlanta.

Comfort and Joy provides, then, a cautiously satisfying ending to the Tote-Crell trilogy. From the squalor of the rooms rented by the Totes to the clean, more-than-sufficient home acquired by Ellen after her life with Bobjay Crell to Dan's loving, nurturing partnership with Ford in their Atlanta home, these novels examined as a whole emphasize individuals' difficult progress, their persistent efforts toward self-improvement, and their attainment of a pragmatic, never idealized, happiness. Examining the novels together also emphasizes the intimacy of the intertwined narratives of Ellen, Dan and, more indirectly, Ford, as they engage in long and hard emotional and psychological journeys to self-acceptance. Although she is a minor character in *Comfort and Joy,* it seems appropriate to note how Ellen's efforts and dreams nonetheless permeate and ripple throughout the novel; consequently, one can read the entire trilogy as an exploration of her strength. The successes that Dan achieves are bolstered by the endurance, fortitude, and flexibility of Ellen herself, a point not meant to diminish Dan's and Ford's own accomplishments. Grimsley published *Comfort and Joy* in English in 1999, roughly three years after the enactment of the Defense of Marriage Act, a perverse misnomer for a fearful and homophobic piece of legislation. Grimsley's published work, particularly this last novel, in its descriptions of Dan and Ford's partnership, provides evidence of and evidence for the need for society's increasing liberalization with regard to class and sexuality. In this vein, despite social and political setbacks and despite the painful limitations on Grimsley's characters' own social progress, *Comfort and Joy* movingly and importantly reflects the resiliency of queer relationships that exist happily and healthily and with hope for the future.

CHAPTER 3

Dream Boy

In between publishing *Winter Birds* (1994) and *My Drowning* (1997), Grimsley published his critically acclaimed *Dream Boy* (1995), and among these three novels similarities resonate strongly. This is in part because they share a close cultural environment, one set near the fictional Potter's Lake, and in part because, as Grimsley himself has noted, "the material of *Winter Birds* carries through into *Dream Boy* and *My Drowning*."[1] Indeed in *Dream Boy* Grimsley expands his depictions of queer rural identities and of domestic abuse and his investigation into how a novel's form can reimagine narrative chronologies and uses of space. While in the Tote-Crell novels he hones these techniques to explore one extended family from an intergenerational perspective, in *Dream Boy* he concentrates them to depict the spiritual, natural, and psychological pleasures and traumas of a burgeoning romance between two adolescent boys, Nathan and Roy. In addition to telling a coming-of-age love story, Grimsley uses his lovers' youth to stress the ambiguities and the confusions manifested in spirituality, in hypocritically rigid religious strictures, in emerging sexualities, and in the distinctions between pleasure and pain. Grimsley enhances the richness of any interpretive process by highlighting the uncertain boundaries between liberatingly dreamlike and too rigidly realistic approaches to the world around us. In doing so, he offers both a physically and a metaphorically tragic hope through refashioning the ancient literary trope of *sparagmos,* a tearing apart that leads to rebirth or to renewal, perhaps most familiar today from the Christian resurrection narrative, and by representing an individual's quest toward self-fulfillment and happiness despite physical and emotional abuse.

While the Tote-Crell books begin by reflecting on natural settings, Grimsley opens *Dream Boy* indoors to highlight how the constraining homophobia of Southern Baptist rigidity, bolstered by secular mores, works to crush the erotic potential and the romance of Christian spiritualism, although not with complete success. Grimsley introduces Nathan as he sits in church listening to his preacher, John Roberts, describe "how at the Last Supper John lay his head tenderly on Jesus's breast." Myopically, the preacher suggests, "we do not know why it is mentioned particularly that Jesus loved John at this moment," and Grimsley makes it clear that his uncertainty stems from a refusal to conceive of a homoerotic history of Christianity, despite his outline of a heightened physical and emotional scenario. Nathan, conversely, intuits an erotic closeness between Jesus and John, and he uses the sermon as an inspiration to daydream about Roy. Indeed, the relationship between these biblical figures provides a structuring device, a safe, spiritually virtuous context that Nathan uses to interpret his desire for the older boy. Listening to the preacher, "Nathan thinks about the body of the son of the farmer who owns the house Nathan's parents rented three weeks ago. Jesus has a face like that boy, a serene smile . . . and Jesus has the same strong, smooth arms" (1–2). The conjoined physical and spiritual language of the sermon provides Nathan with a legitimizing rhetoric and a perspective, albeit one unintended by the preacher, with which to understand his fascination with Roy's physicality and his personality, his kind, calm strength.

While Nathan initially reflects on Roy in spiritualized physical terms, Grimsley quickly extends the boys' powerful mutual attraction into more everyday natural contexts. After Nathan arrives at Roy's school, Roy unexpectedly starts drawing closer to him, leading his friends Burke and Randy out of their "usual territory" to eat lunch with Nathan and to follow him afterward as "if by accident," which thrills Nathan (7, 8). Grimsley quickly imbues this seemingly accidental exploration with rationally, then scientifically explainable motivations. Although Roy is a senior and Nathan a sophomore, Roy uses Nathan's academic reputation—Nathan has skipped a grade—to ask for help with an English essay, after which for repayment and to spend more time together Roy teaches Nathan algebra (6). Grimsley uses algebra as a metaphor to characterize the boys' longings for each other as logically, even as physiologically inspired. Roy "sets out problems" for Nathan, symbolizing overtly mathematical and metaphorically social problems, "that become increasingly clear" with "a solution" discoverable via "a peculiar and inexorable logic." Tellingly, "enlightenment comes to Nathan at the same time that Roy's presence begins to have its usual effect on him" as "X and Y hang in the air between them" (21–22). These algebraic symbols for unknown variables explicitly recall the male sex chromosomes and, by extension, these boys' genetic predisposition to same-sex attraction, a previously unknown variable in their relationship. The symbols also evoke variables that can logically be defined by the boys' peculiar, because unconventional, and inexorable physical, emotional, even psychological desires for each other's presence. Mathematics and nature combine to present a problem but also to legitimate the boys' love as a vital part of their lives and the biological world. This algebraic metaphor also anticipates the potential for the discovery of solutions to the boys' problems as social conditioning and nature dialectically shape and reshape human responses.

One solution is to escape from restrictive human-made structures to more private natural shelters outdoors, which allows a spiritualized physical eroticism unencumbered by the religious strictures selectively enforced at home or at church. While Nathan and Roy first draw physically close in Nathan's bedroom after studying algebra, they run outside to explore the intensity of their newfound relationship. Hidden by trees, they undress, and one kneels near the other in a position of sensually charged prayer (26). Later that week the boys explore the nearby woods and fields, which provide them with the freedom to undress and to sing Cleland McAfee's hymn "Near to the Heart of God," before embracing and kissing (42). If the boys remain somewhat suspicious of what they hear in their respective homes and churches—Roy jokes that according to his preacher "pretty much everything you can do is wrong . . . especially if it's fun" (50)—they take spirituality seriously. Their time outdoors enables them to pursue the "peculiar and inexorable logic" of their feelings for each other in intensely joyful and seemingly sanctified natural settings that bring them, they feel, closer to each other's heart and to a divine presence.

This spiritualized nature provides some resistance to overt religious failures, particularly in Nathan's family, and to more harmful human desires. Outside, Nathan and Roy can sing "Near to the Heart of God," recalling its line "a place where sin cannot molest," a line that Grimsley leaves unquoted but that he employs by implication, as a sort of overtone, to characterize the boys' sinless, perhaps even holy relationship.[2] Nathan's family's constant attention to Baptist morals, conversely, remains pointedly unable to protect their family from sexual abuse. In church, Nathan's mother can dream "of a Sunday morning that will never end," because her husband, Harland, will not get drunk and molest Nathan in the public space where they spend these mornings. Yet this church-inspired safety is severely limited. Invitations to "the Men's Prayer Circle on Tuesday," "the Deacons' Breakfast on Saturday," "Wednesday Prayer Meeting[s]," among other church-sponsored events, in addition to frequent Bible readings at home, fail to stop Harland from drinking too much and from increasingly ogling Nathan (2, 3). For his family, this attention recalls Harland's previous molestation of his son. Consequently, when not in church, Nathan's mother "moves as if she would like to be invisible" and remains perpetually distant from everyone (14). Guilt-ridden over being unable to shield Nathan and unwarrantedly ashamed of her inability to satisfy Harland sexually, Nathan's mother eventually "cannot look [Nathan] in the eye any longer" (3). When Harland refocuses on Nathan, starting a new cycle of abuse, she withdraws further into herself as Nathan flees from home to sleep in the woods near where he first kissed Roy. Harland's alcoholism and uncontrollable desires destroy his wife's psyche and her sense of agency—we are not even told her name, indicating her intense longing to disappear—and he terrifies his son. Harland's behavior exhibits an unfortunate because harmful sexuality. Grimsley also, however, uses Harland to indict the impotence of conservative Baptist culture to deal helpfully with sexuality in all its varieties. To safeguard a family only during church services provides a horrifically ironic level of protection for an allegedly divine organization, even if it is restricted by human imperfections.

Still, Grimsley avoids idealizing a natural spiritual space in opposition to more pervasively institutional or social structures. Social traditions frequently infiltrate and fuse with natural environments to create a supernatural aura of crime and rejection that troubles the evolving relationship between Nathan and Roy. The boys spend most of their time together traversing what Ellen Crowell has called Grimsley's "gothic Eden," specifically land protectively hidden by trees and foliage that used to belong to the Kennicutt plantation and that provides an intensely ironic "refuge from the violence of the present" in the remnants of the South's violent past for their romantic explorations.[3] Crowell's reading works in conjunction with Michael Bibler's demonstration of how, despite what one might expect, plantations in mid-twentieth-century literature often create "an intrinsically queer cultural space" in the South.[4] Ed Madden suggests, analogously, that Grimsley's late twentieth-century *Dream Boy* uses an antebellum plantation setting to evoke the "vicious enactment" of racism, misogyny, and homophobia but also to indicate a "place where homoeroticism may be transformed into healing."[5] To a degree, Grimsley does use southern gothic tropes of plantations, of aristocratic decay amid rural beauty, of taboo sexual relationships, of heightened excitement, and of pervasive fears in hidden spaces to evoke Edenic refuges and spaces of queerness and healing, but he also, and perhaps predominantly, uses these spaces to evoke the long-standing social obstacles that fuse into his lovers' natural desires. The boys kneel in protective grass and brush outside the constraints of home and church, but they do so in a cemetery left behind by a faded slave-owning family, and Roy insists here that Nathan "can't tell" anyone about their relationship, a version of dehumanization reminiscent, however faintly, of slavery (28–29). The boys, moreover, come together not just for sex but for closeness and warmth, yet to do so safely they lie "trembling and huddle[d] together" in "the dark of [a] grave," a huge obelisk that covers them from view (22, 23, 26–27). Wonderful desires get dampened by a once grandiose but far from extinct social conservativism recalling to the boys persistent promises of the metaphorical death of their everyday lives if they get discovered and the reputed tortures of the damnation promised after death for those who flout religious strictures (50). Understandably, their physical reaction is to tremble with desire and with fear simultaneously.

The intensity and the stifling of the boys' spiritualized desires mutually increase when they go camping with Randy and Burke on a journey to the Kennicutts' last decaying plantation house, which had once dominated the surroundings and which nature is working to reclaim. While the boys walk, the woods become "a kind of church, requiring reverence," "a green- and gold-leafed choir," and at night a "mansion of dusk and rain collapsing," where during a storm Roy and Nathan satisfy the aforementioned requirement for reverence by revering each other, making love in a tent, a sweet tension that results in Nathan making Roy "laugh and cry out loud" (112, 120, 122). The woods take on the protective and noble aura of a sanctum or grand house, a correspondent to a plantation house but one fit for ecstasy and heaven-pleasing noises, natural and human-made constructions blurring. This environment, however, offers simply a temporary, collapsing protection as the boys remain hidden from the allegedly sanctified constraints of heteronormativity only while the storm falls and its noises isolate them from their schoolmates, who sleep in a separate tent. The end goal of the plantation lingers, meanwhile, as a symbol of social oppression, rotting but still dominating, to remind them of the need to hide. Life mingles with death and turbulence as Roy and Nathan understandably try to hide their spiritual and physical attraction for each other, which all too obviously overwhelms them. A sense of danger and decay consequently invades their sheltered space, as evidenced by Roy's continued insistence on a protective secrecy.

While Roy grapples primarily with his need for secrecy, Nathan must learn to associate same-sex desire with loving interactions between partners rather than with incestuous abuse. Nathan works hard to distinguish between diverse manifestations of same-sex eroticism, to reinterpret similar behaviors that assume drastically different meanings stemming from different intentions. This takes an intense mental effort on Nathan's part. "Sometimes the look in Roy's eyes," Grimsley reports, "reminds Nathan . . . of the look in his own father's eyes, but Nathan prefers not to think about that" (4). During this process, he realizes, "in a fleeting way, the irony that what pleases him with Roy terrifies him with his father" (101). One strategy is thus for Nathan to erect mental barriers that block thoughts of his father while he is with Roy in order to reject the similarities between their looks, touches, and longings. Similarly, Nathan has to separate Roy's protective desire for secrecy after sex and its implication of Roy's homophobic guilt from his own reluctance to think about his father's abuse, which, while Nathan has done nothing wrong, understandably makes him uncomfortable and even feel, unwarrantedly, guilty himself (55). Finally, Nathan has to disassociate his and Roy's unwarranted sense of guilt for consensual sex from Harland's warranted guilt for raping Nathan.

A second strategy is for Nathan to use cautiously his knowledge, however unhappily gained, in beneficial ways as he and Roy grow more physically intimate. Nathan wants to please both Roy and himself, but he fears demonstrating too quickly his sexual experience and fears Roy's curiosity regarding it. Consequently, Nathan learns to "balance between what he knows and what he should not know" as he dreads both his own memories of his father and Roy's rejection should he learn of the incestuous relationship. Harland's abuse therefore disrupts Nathan's sexual maturation and his longing to be honest with Roy. One afternoon, after the boys "cling and press until they finish" in orgasm, Roy asks if Nathan has done "this before with anybody," and Nathan dissembles by omission: "Nathan shakes his head. . . . He has never liked it before. That much is true" (35). When pressed, however, he overtly lies, causing him to feel "hollow inside" (36). Nathan knows about sexual encounters between men, and so he tries to use his experience to please Roy and himself, but any discussion of sex generally leaves Nathan feeling uneasy. As such, the physically, spiritually, psychologically, and emotionally joyous coming together between the boys becomes fraught with misunderstandings and evasion because of Harland.

Roy's willingness, despite his own fears and frustrations, to care for Nathan nonetheless helps Nathan to differentiate between the boys' and Harland's desires. Grimsley indicates this differentiation structurally by consistently positioning analogous scenes in proximity to each other to emphasize how versions of male physicality acquire oppositional meanings for Nathan depending upon sympathy and consent. Early in the novel, after Nathan has rejoiced in being with Roy in the woods "dressed only in white underwear" while their physical and emotional "warmth makes chromosomes sing," Nathan returns home to find his father "wearing his white boxer shorts with the stained front," his shirt torn, his flesh repulsive, the result of excessive drinking stemming from the self-loathing and mental stress caused by his coercive sexual encounters with his son (27, 30). This second meeting gruesomely echoes the consensual, caring scene in the woods. Roy could always potentially become like Harland, this echo suggests, but he repeatedly avoids this, even at his most angry. After Nathan's mother warns Nathan one afternoon to stay away from Harland, who is once again becoming abusive, Nathan introduces Roy to anal sex as a means to reclaim his own sexuality, as a pleasure to share, and to conquer Roy's own fear of isolation by getting as close to him as physically possible (73). Unfortunately this sharing backfires, and the boys "finish in violence, straining and sour." What Nathan intended as an empowering intimacy fills Roy with horror and suspicion. "Who taught you how to screw like that," Roy asks as he gets a "savage look in his eyes," his "grip on Nathan's arm tightens," he "raises his hand," and Nathan flinches and cowers (74). Their evening closes with Roy sitting silently in his car, crying (75). Roy's actions evoke how blurry the line is between gripping someone in passionate love and doing so in anger with an intention to hurt, between desire and confusion. Still, Roy noticeably switches from savagery to tears, which offers some solace to Nathan. For Nathan recalls his mother's warning, and Grimsley follows this scene in the car with Nathan's fearful return home and Harland's invasion of Nathan's bedroom that night and the next, Nathan twice fleeing before his father can catch him. In the car, Nathan anticipates these invasions, and it is telling that the boys' overall intimacy still allows him to feel that Roy is a source of protection even as they drive home in silent dejection (74). Nathan senses that Roy, himself anxious and crying, cares about him enough not to hurt him like his father does and to be a source of strength for him despite their differences in how to interpret their intimacy.

These difficulties and the boys' responses to them illustrate the complex anxieties and the halting progression of Grimsley's characters toward self-fulfillment, a form of Grimsley's own pragmatic optimism. Previously Roy has been quiet or exhibited coldness toward Nathan after physical intimacy as he has accustomed himself cautiously to their new situation before drawing closer still to Nathan (20, 32). Roy has liked their sex too much, it being too much male-male intimacy for him to accept easily, especially as he suspects that Nathan has had sex previously with someone else. Roy obsesses over keeping his relationship with Nathan private, partially for self-preservation but also to imagine that they are attracted to each other specifically, not to men in general. Nathan's having had sex with other men would undermine Roy's limited understanding and his sense of general normalcy. If Nathan desires men in general, then Roy, who desires Nathan, might likewise. Roy may also fear that if Nathan has desired others enough to have sex with them, then Nathan might abandon Roy, leaving him alone to face social hostility. All this funnels into Roy's horror (74). But, unlike Harland, Roy fights this selfish reaction, especially when he recognizes both the intimacy that Nathan has shared and the reality that Nathan has been forced from his home and so is experiencing more immediate problems than Roy himself. Without asking questions, Roy searches out Nathan in the graveyard, where they first knelt together and where

Nathan therefore feels safe. Subsequently, as Roy hides Nathan in his family's barn, they pass a week in tense safety, their relationship growing stronger after their conflict, largely because of their physical and emotional closeness: "They talk with their bodies. Roy says he is sorry again and again and never makes a sound" (105). Undoubtedly this silence problematically distracts from largely unsolvable difficulties: they are young, they have not finished school, and they have little money; they would be separated by authorities if they sought help; and they are still getting used to their love, individually and as a couple. Nonetheless, this ability to forget their difficulties makes room for them to fortify their relationship. Roy makes Nathan feel safe, and they offer each other shelter and protection (35, 36). They use this closeness to overcome outside obstacles to their relationship, as they increasingly understand their erotic connections to be evidence of their mutual emotional and psychological needs and a chance for joy rather than as sin or a shameful joining.

While Roy and Nathan offer a pragmatically optimistic example of youthful romance, one filled with excitement, tenderness, and sympathy, their schoolmate Burke embodies a more aggressively repressed male eroticism. Initially, this manifests itself in brutal play and misogyny. Burke frequently "likes to be too rough" with Randy, whom he once pretends "to drown," taking the pretense "too far" and nearly causing a fight (133, 67). Simultaneous longings for dominance, human touch, and excitement, all unexamined, cause Burke to hurt his friend. Burke similarly pursues a heightened antagonism toward women, one undoubtedly exacerbated by the constraints on the social and economic equality of women in U.S. society. When Randy sex-shames a local girl behind her back, calling her "pretty much" a whore to deceive himself and the others into feeling sophisticated and adult, Burke amplifies the already cruel conversation by observing, "might as well stick your hand in a cow pussy," a dehumanization and imagined violation that causes the boys, except Nathan, to laugh (70). Grimsley critiques the aggressive discussions of women that too frequently characterize public and semipublic masculine conversations. He stresses, moreover, how the most frightened, violent, and extreme voices can control a conversation as Burke takes the lead and as Nathan, understandably and yet lamentably, stays quiet, a too subtle example of resistance.

Grimsley uses the boys' conversation to evoke the need to resist socially facilitated misogyny, which he also carefully connects here to systematic forms of racism. Indeed, Grimsley suggests thematically and structurally how one form of prejudice can influence another by having the boys' degradation of the girl follow earlier references to racial integration in the same paragraph. The boys go to school in the aftermath of federally mandated racial integration in Potter's Lake, likely in the mid-1960s, when Grimsley's own childhood school became integrated in North Carolina. On a previous afternoon, Roy has talked openly about this process and avowed to Nathan "that the black kids are okay if you get to know them" (16). Roy's perspective signals his burgeoning acknowledgment of the humanity of diverse social groups despite local social pressures that insist on racial divisions. While homophobia, misogyny, and racism are of course different problems with unique difficulties, Grimsley usefully recalls their shared ideological foundations in an irrational fearful hate. He does so to highlight how resistance against one form of intolerance can and should encourage resistance against others, even if resistance rarely works in this ideal fashion. Roy, for instance, fails to defend the girl Burke dehumanizes, and although he considers "black kids" to be okay, we never read of him or Nathan interacting with African American individuals, suggesting that the African Americans among their schoolmates and neighbors are not a major part of the boys' everyday consciousness, even though they should be as part of their community. Still, Grimsley implies that Roy's mindset with regard to race facilitates or contextualizes his recognition of a diverse humanity in ways that allow him to consider his relationship with Nathan less antagonistically, if not unproblematically, and leaves him open to engaging racial conflicts in the future.

Burke, conversely, evidences the losses and the unresisted resentment stemming from the systemic racism taught by his father, who himself echoes large swathes of American society. Burke, for instance, would play "football except the team is mostly black and his dad won't let him play with blacks" (70). As in the Tote-Crell trilogy, while most harmful to African Americans, racism rarely works out well for nonaffluent white characters, and Burke's inherited racism causes him to miss out on a sport that he wants to play and encourages bitterness that erupts into further general intolerance. This bitterness is suggested when almost immediately following Burke's reference to his halted football career his anger displaces itself through his degrading comment about the young woman in his conversation with Roy, Randy, and Nathan. Analogously, Grimsley uses Burke's increasingly aggressive stance toward Roy and Nathan as they move toward the old plantation house on their camping trip to assert that the mentalities that foster socially permissible aggressions against vulnerable groups, here women, African Americans, and queer individuals, are linked and the consequent need for a multifaceted resistance to diverse social intolerances.

Of course, it should be noted, using racial integration and prejudice to contextualize a narrative focused on white homosexuality risks eliding black history and experiences. African Americans are frequently mentioned in *Dream Boy*, for instance, but are never fully present within the novel, somewhat akin to the boys' mothers and female acquaintances. In other works, such as *My Drowning*, *Winter Birds*, *Boulevard*, and *How I Shed My Skin*, Grimsley provides more balanced casts to achieve his different thematic and aesthetic purposes. In *Dream Boy*, nonetheless, he does work hard to indicate that if women and African Americans are not at the forefront of these boys' minds, their vital presence permeates these boys' lives. He offers this context to emphasize how the cultural pervasiveness of racial prejudice, past and present, often works in conjunction with sexual and gender prejudices, an association that society must recognize if it is to redress it. If through Roy in particular Grimsley suggests how these prejudices can begin to be overcome as certain human interactions encourage a rethinking of analogous relationships, albeit much too slowly, then through Burke Grimsley suggests how a general ideology of fear, anger, and repression can overflow and manifest in resentment and violence in a variety of specific yet interconnected arenas. Burke's resentment of his inability to play football because of his father's racism, added to his resentment of his inability to pursue his erotic interests due to general sexual repression in his Southern Baptist society, overflows into a frustrated cruelty toward Randy, Roy, Nathan, and unnamed girls. For Burke, social repressions and a conflicting longing to engage others intimately lead to feelings of guilt and confusion, which he counters with a compensatory belligerence to reassert his social dominance. Thus, Grimsley insists on these ideological links between aggressive, socially constructed rural masculinities and repressions of intimacy along a whole continuum of platonic and erotic relationships.

Grimsley's primary focus with Burke, nonetheless, is to show how his frustrations and assertions of social dominance result in sexual aggression. Burke both pursues and distances himself from same-sex eroticism through increasingly heightened displays of a physically and psychologically forceful masculinity. Nathan recognizes a "rivalry between Roy and Burke," which on Burke's side stems from envy of Roy's charisma, an envy intensified by an unwilling and secret attraction to Roy (63). When the boys go on their trip to the abandoned plantation house, the journey gives Burke the opportunity to discern the closeness between Roy and Nathan. Resentful of this relationship, Burke tries to humiliate Roy and to make him jealous by attracting Nathan to himself by showing Nathan increased attention and by displays of his more mature body. On the second day of the trip, Burke subverts Roy's physical and metaphorical leadership of the group by walking "closer to Nathan," so near that "Nathan can almost feel" Burke's "breath on his neck" (128). Subsequently, Burke stands so that Roy and Randy cannot see him, and, as he "watches Nathan," he remarks how hot it is, takes off his shirt, and shows off his arms, which are "thick and brawny" as he "stretches them upward," "still watching" Nathan (129–30). Disconcerted by this private display, which Burke's sustained gaze indicates is pointedly aimed at Nathan, Nathan is embarrassed by his own interest in Burke and the consequent implication of his disloyalty to Roy (130). In an interview, Grimsley has remarked that Burke represents a "darkly dangerous sexual being," a persona that Grimsley explored in greater depth in *Boulevard* and that in *Dream Boy* becomes temporarily fascinating to Nathan as it works in opposition to his more healthy relationship with Roy.[6] Despite this fascination, Nathan ultimately shifts closer to Roy, preferring his strong softness and their mutual care (130). This rejection stings Burke, who turns to whiskey as a consolation, drinking earlier in the day than either Roy or Randy will in order to bolster his sense of maturity while also dulling his insecurities, thereby allowing him to challenge Roy more aggressively. Burke starts walking closer to Roy and "displaying his broad bare shoulders, like a challenge," and he even "winks at Nathan over Roy's head" (132, 137). Burke attempts to overshadow Roy and to draw Nathan into a private collusion, his precise intentions remaining safely undefined, arguably friendly or playful rather than erotic, and so not exactly taboo, even as he clearly exhibits predatory behaviors.

While physical interactions are progressively more supportive between Roy and Nathan, between Burke and others they become progressively more sadistic. As Burke feels repeatedly rejected and isolated, he reveals the homophobic cruelty that can erupt from a repressed adolescent sexuality. After the four boys enter the plantation house on the second evening of their trip, noises and shadows frighten them, and Burke and Randy separate from Roy and Nathan. Nathan grows uncannily attuned to and engrossed by the preternatural morbidity of the abandoned house, which brings together the ghosts of past racial violence, religious strictures, his own father, and fears that Roy himself will treat Nathan too roughly. With a "plaintive note," Roy begs Nathan not to focus on whatever he senses, and, to distract Nathan, Roy performs oral sex for him for the first time, what Nathan will later consider a "miracle of reciprocity" (163, 165). In the midst of this comforting act of unity, Burke and Randy rejoin the boys and realize the extent of their relationship. Disgust is Randy's response, and this socially conditioned reaction likewise informs Burke's bitterness at his contradictory mélange of jealousy, longing, and a desire to humiliate Roy, all released in Burke's yearning taunt "looks like Roy sucks dick pretty good" and his command "don't stop now" as "Roy shoves Nathan away" (164). Burke's anger flares because Nathan and Roy have chosen each other for protection and pleasure rather than Burke, who cannot openly acknowledge his longing for same-sex intimacy. This rejection intensifies Burke's anger at his unwanted attraction to men and his desire to take Roy or Nathan's place or at least to watch, as he really does not want Roy to stop. These confused emotions cause sex to become, for Burke, a mercenary means to humiliate others while fueling covertly his ultimately unsatisfied desires for physical and emotional closeness.

Indeed, Burke's confirmation of his suspicions regarding Roy and Nathan horrifically amplifies his volatile mixture of homophobic and homoerotic outbursts. Roy, Randy, and Burke initially flee from Nathan to avoid dealing with the situation, but Burke returns, grabs and hits Nathan, takes him to the mansion's attic, drinks more whiskey, then beats him again before making a complex plea for Nathan's affection. "Don't pull away from me," Burke demands in a "plaintive" tone, perversely echoing Roy's earlier "plaintive note" and the lovers' interrupted togetherness (169–70). "Roy left you . . . I came back," Burke stresses, making a perverse claim for his own fidelity, after which he jealously recounts seeing the oral sex downstairs. When Nathan nonetheless attempts to distract his assailant by suggesting that they return to the camp, this rejection "enrages Burke," who rapes Nathan and then knocks him half-conscious (170). Grimsley's brief yet vivid description of the rape illustrates how intensely and dangerously eroticism and violence can intertwine as Burke's initially attractive body becomes an instrument of torture and orifices with the potential for pleasure each become a wound (172). Burke's drunken aggression and subsequent misery fulfill Nathan's chief fear, namely the possibility of a closeness that is callous, degrading, and self-loathing (173). Burke thus resonates with a variety of figures in Nathan's life, such as his father, even though young adult homosexuality differs from pedophilia; with his preacher's refusal to recognize the romantic love between Jesus and John; and with the boys' rural society's general repudiation of consensual same-sex encounters even though such encounters have always existed within almost any given community. Burke's loathing-infused lust is, like his racism, a pervasive inheritance, bequeathed and intensified by his environment in ways that harm everyone involved.

Grimsley expands and historicizes Burke's invidious social resonances by placing the novel within a southern gothic tradition that uses supernatural occurrences to link the past to the present and the future. These gothic links magnify abstract connections between diverse aggressions, particularly sexual aggressions, and their individual extensions from what might be called a more general will to cruelty.[7] The novel's haunted plantation mansion exists as a symbol of elegance that has decayed because it was built on a rotten, unjust foundation, predominantly slavery but also socioeconomic inequality, misogyny, and sexual prejudices, all injustices that continue into the present and that show only slight signs of abating. Grimsley emphasizes this nexus of injustice as the boys explore the house after sunset and encounter a ghostly figure that they associate first with the last master of the plantation, who "got killed by one of his slaves" and whom Nathan subsequently sees as a "vaguer shadow," one that looks "like Nathan's Dad when he was younger, like Preacher John

Roberts. Like Roy," yet who is also "another blankness of the house, a ghost who could be anyone, living or dead" (136, 161). This figure allows Grimsley to evoke how a vaguer line of general cruelty manifests into specific forms that stem from or echo past injustices. Hence, in the house, the passage of time seems to have "been slowed or stopped" (141). This play with time evokes the multiple ways that the past extends into the present and the abstract into the personal and the particular.

Grimsley further complicates the timeline of his narrative as he indicates that each past and present event anticipates an array of futures that might be diversely realized in parallel or analogous sequences. Grimsley has remarked that he has used the present tense in *Dream Boy* to characterize Nathan as "being absorbed in the moment" and "removed from what had happened in his past." In order to normalize his life, as Grimsley himself has suggested, Nathan has to "continue thinking in the present tense."[8] In the mansion, however, Grimsley multiplies this "present tense" into myriad simultaneous presents that draw obsessively on the past and on the future to absorb Nathan into equally valid realities. Grimsley describes, for instance, how when Nathan reencounters the ghostly figure in the house, one "moment broadens" and "divides. . . . There are two of Nathan, moving in different directions," and Nathan both follows the figure as it moves "up the stairs . . . through ceilings . . . upward into the air, into heaven" and remains with the figure in the house (161). With the figure representing, in part, his father, Nathan experiences diverse abuses both killing him, a sacrifice that gains him a final spiritual peace, and holding him in limbo in the living death of the morbid mansion. More optimistically, Roy gives himself to Nathan at this moment to demonstrate how the past can also evolve into a positive future. Grimsley's characterization of time here reaffirms how the past and the future both fuse into the present, as the hope of a present and a future with Roy allows Nathan's mind to expand more willing into times to come. When Roy flees, Roy jeopardizes this future and re-evokes for Nathan past and anticipated betrayals by his family, religion, and society, all of which should protect but which actively hurt him and which will do so again, most immediately through their embodiment in Burke.

By emphasizing two of Nathan's chief divisions and by utilizing a surreal configuration of time that allows for parallel narratives for the same individual, Grimsley prepares for a conclusion that encourages at least three predominating interpretations of the results of Burke's beating of Nathan. This beating occurs at the end of chapter 12, well toward the final pages of the novel but at the midpoint of its twenty-four chapters. This structure enables a long powerful build-up to what becomes the formal center of the novel and the first of two climaxes, the second of which follows quickly when Nathan reunites with

Roy. These dual climaxes strongly imply both that Burke kills Nathan, even if Nathan is possibly resurrected spiritually or physically, and that Nathan survives to reunite with Roy.[9] These seemingly oppositional interpretations might most accurately be read as a blend of realism and surrealism, in the sense of a dreamlike, heightened state of being. This fusing creates a third reading that holds these two interpretations in a bittersweet tension, one hovering between earthly happiness destroyed and earthly happiness fulfilled, neither interpretation complete without the other, and providing a Keatsian negative capability, a rejection of a need for certainty, which allows both results to exist simultaneously as accurate.

From one perspective, then, we should interpret this formally central act of rape and beating as Burke prevailing over the boys by killing Nathan. Jealous and vengeful, Burke extends the plantation's past cultural violence to the present by extracting sexual pleasure from Roy's lover, a substitute for Roy himself, and by punishing Nathan for being Roy's lover. He prevents the two from reuniting in life while he concurrently eliminates the only witness to his own queerness by hitting Nathan so hard that a "hole opens" in his head and "the wind touches his brain" (174). There is tragedy in this fatal wound and in Burke's ability to convince Nathan that this is his fate, that, having been abused since childhood, he deserves to be abused and that everyone knows it: "both he and Burke understand that he is made for this use. . . . Dad opened a hole in Nathan, and now anyone can use it" (172). Nathan's misconception results from horrific, seemingly interconnected circumstances, including his father's abuse, Roy's abandonment, Burke's sadism, and a general social intolerance, all of which lead him to conflate his desire for men with a belief that he is destined for pain and degradation. This seeming fate destroys Nathan's sense of agency, which is reproduced in his probable physical death. While Grimsley never explicitly identifies Nathan as lifeless, the next morning, in chapter 13, Roy and Randy find him, and Randy suggests that he's dead (176). Crying, Roy covers Nathan with a shroudlike cloth, and Nathan's ghostly consciousness hovers over his cold body that "cannot move" and that is found in the "afternoon light" in chapter 14 by his father and "other men" with a "crackling of a radio," presumably the sheriff, mentioned later by Roy, and his deputies (176, 177–78, 193). This evidence almost incontrovertibly indicates Nathan's murder, his death confirmed by a schoolmate, his lover, and authority figures. Nathan thus transforms into yet another ghost to haunt the house, the nearby woods, and, subsequently, Roy's dreams.

In this reading, the twelve final chapters become a surreal sequence emphasizing a spiritual rather than a material presence in life. Nathan reawakens in a ghostly state and wanders outside near where Burke took off his shirt, where

"Burke will be watching the road. It will be his image, it will always linger. It will wait for Nathan, it will wish for Roy" (184). At places of trauma, of dangerous attraction, such ghostly images will remain impressed, waiting and re-meeting even during the day, recalling the daytime ghosts discussed earlier by Randy (140). Simultaneously, Nathan continues walking to meet Roy, traversing places of significance to them like stations of the cross—the campsite, certain fields, the cemetery—until he finds Roy outside his church, where the boys rejoin each other. Roy goes to Nathan, and they run to the woods, a reminder of their first afternoon together in the cemetery, although now the specter of death takes greater prominence. "You were dead," Roy informs Nathan, and he "examines the wound in Nathan's skull," with a distracted dreamlike quality to his behavior, before noting ". . . anyhow. Our preacher preached this evening about how the dead will rise" (194, 195). Here, as Ed Madden has convincingly argued, Grimsley's novel "reworks the Southern gothic as a reconfigured gospel, thus moving from the return of the repressed to the return of [the] resurrected . . . to reinscribe a positive homoeroticism within Southern homophobia" using "the language and symbolism of Christian traditions."[10] Still, amid this optimism, it is important not to lose sight of what has happened to get to this point. This reunion is joyous, but its spiritual surrealism, the gothic as gospel, the familiar Christian promise of resurrection coming true that explains Roy's seemingly nonchalant response to Nathan's reappearance, maintains a distinctly tragic perspective. If Burke has killed Nathan, then the boys can be together only via a miracle brought about by a sacrifice, Nathan's physical death, which symbolizes, at the very least, queer bodies sacrificed to heteronormativity. Or, the boys can be together only in a supernatural world outside reality, perhaps in Roy's distracted dreams of Nathan's resurrection, Nathan literally becoming Roy's dream boy. Grimsley has noted, albeit in a speculative tense, that "in spite of the ending," "whatever life they have, it seems to me, it's out of the world as we know it."[11] Whether this refers to a shared life after death, Grimsley leaves unclear, but joy here is predicated on fatal violence, regardless of any bodily resurrection.

With regards to an alternative reading, while Grimsley gives ample evidence that Nathan has died, the novel also implies that Nathan defies Burke by remaining barely alive and then recovering. In this reading, Nathan's consciousness in chapter 13 is not ghostly but survives in a body that is too cold, too scared, too exhausted, and, most emphatically, "too sore to move," so that Roy and Randy, who themselves are exhausted and scared and who can barely bring themselves to look at Nathan lying on the floor, miss his weak signs of life before leaving for home and the authorities. Subsequently, in a daze Nathan mistakes the morning light for "afternoon light" in chapter 14. In this daze, as he hovers between life and death, the "voices of people everywhere, on every side, black voices and white voices, echoing," as well as the vision of Harland, are all those of ghosts, echoes of the past, or, if one insists on a reality without apparitions, part of the "dream" Nathan suspects he has as he awaits the "quiet whiteness" of an oncoming death (177, 178). Only a sudden vision of Roy averts this death, as it "fills Nathan with a longing he can hardly contain" and revives him (178). Grimsley's evocation of haunting presences in the house and elsewhere signify, in this case, less phantasms and more ineradicable memories that get displaced by the force of Nathan's still tenuous corporeal presence (184). Attempting to escape the plantation, "he is afraid he will not be able to leave the attic," and he seems surprised when the "doorknob, solid to his touch, turns" (179). Grimsley's syntax indicates that Nathan fears that his body is an apparition and thus seems surprised not only that the doorknob is solid but that his hand is solid and does not go through the doorknob.

Grimsley maintains a suspension even at this point—is Nathan a spirit with a supernaturally materialized presence or is he conventionally alive?—and he offers a relief only when Nathan begins to take charge of his future. A decision to have more of a say over his life, Grimsley suggests, preferably but not necessarily with Roy, revitalizes Nathan physically. When Nathan reencounters Roy outside the latter's church in chapter 23, he tells Roy he is leaving, and this jolts the uncertain Roy into touching Nathan in order to slow him, momentarily. At this point, Nathan is at last "certain he still has a body. . . . It is a relief that they can feel each other . . . that they are in the same world" (193). Grimsley never identifies specifically that this "same world" is the conventional world of the living. But, this merger of Nathan's reassertion of agency over his life, moving Roy to touch him, and Nathan's corporeality strongly imply that Nathan's fear of being dead is unrealized. Descriptions of Nathan haunting places are thus metaphorical, poetic references to memory. The boys will have therefore a chance to attempt a physically, emotionally, spiritually, and psychologically fulfilling relationship. No matter how troubled or tenuous, interpretations of these chapters according to a contemporary realism, one skeptical of apparitions, provide a powerfully optimistic ending.

With these final scenes, Grimsley reminds us that continued life enables second and third chances that can decay or strengthen relationships. As Nathan's father "goes through cycles" that confirm his grotesqueness, so Roy and Nathan go together through converse cycles consisting of disappointments countered and overcome by memories of how they love each other, work and learn well together, and want to protect each other, which increasingly renew their mutual commitment (58). They remember how so soon after they met, "Roy's chores suddenly require[d] Nathan's presence, and Roy's homework beg[ged] Nathan's help," and how this foundation facilitated their ability to listen to and to support each other (51). As a result, the boys grow so close that at times they feel "as if either of them could contain, for the moment, the consciousness of both . . . echoing in each other" (55–56). Thus, when Nathan decides to leave Potter's Lake, saying, "I don't think I can stay here," Roy follows him, choosing to stay with Nathan rather than to abandon him as he did in the plantation house, a decision Roy signals by taking Nathan's hand (192, 193). Both boys make positive, active decisions that draw on and surpass the significance of previous ones: Nathan decides not to become invisible like his mother, and Roy decides not to reject again what he wants most. The boys' cyclical experiences, much like those between Dan and Ford in *Comfort and Joy*, allow them to reaffirm less their betrayals, miscommunications, and fears than how well they can coexist with increasing intimacy and joy in life.

Still, the boys' ability to hold in common and to negotiate diverse memories suggests that to divide Grimsley's ending into two possible readings concerned with death or life and then to consider these readings as mutually exclusive, or one certainly right and the other certainly wrong, is to miss his point. Tracing diverse interpretations of conflicting evidence is a necessary step to see how Grimsley's style, his form and his language, allows Nathan to be both dead and living, with Grimsley encouraging us to hold these two key readings in tandem. The division of Nathan's return journey (from the attic room to the campsite where the boys made love to the final scenes outside Roy's church) into extremely short chapters highlights the discontinuity of the narrative and the relatively parallel timelines that occur simultaneously in the text, what Nathan senses as "lines dividing" (177). These semantic, thematic, and structurally parallel lines enable Grimsley to present multiple possibilities concurrently: Nathan dies and does not die; he is resurrected literally and only metaphorically; he believes he is responsible for his abuse and learns that he is not; he confirms that sex is pain and accepts that sex can be loving, safe, exciting, and shame-free; he haunts this world passively and takes agency in it, with myriad composite possibilities between each of these extremes.

Yet, a novel must end somewhere, and Grimsley ends *Dream Boy* by optimistically focusing on those possible lines that reunite the boys rather than those, for instance, that take Nathan to heaven and leave Roy on earth alone. As such, Grimsley offers a bittersweet tragedy with a forward-looking resolution, since in these lines both boys move toward a more accurate comprehension of nature and spirituality. When the boys rest briefly under a gingko tree, the leaves fall, as ginkgo leaves will, like "a snowdrift of saffron and amber" around them. Roy "pulls Nathan against him and for a while they become one flesh." Roy grows "rapt . . . as if he is blossoming, a flower opening," while

Nathan remembers his preacher's confusion at "the Disciple John resting his head on Jesus's chest," a gesture that Nathan reproduces here with Roy as he now understands its meaning of homoerotic intimacy (194–95). This is not a queering of nature or spirituality but an experientially verified realization that they have always already been queer, queer meaning homoerotic as well as expansive and different from we have been taught. The boys' love is natural, spiritual, and the start of a new beginning, and it is a significant advantage that a novel can end so that we need not concentrate too hard on how both boys will leave home without a high school diploma, without money, without much knowledge of the world outside their rural environment, and without a plan except for clinging to each other.

The boys' love might, nonetheless, survive even these quite serious hardships. This may seem a surrealistic or dreamlike prediction, but Grimsley consistently reminds us that the difference between surrealism and a conventional realism is only a matter of interpretation and an evolved sensitivity. While he certainly heightens the dreamlike nature of the novel at its end, he consistently intersperses surrealistic moments throughout the narrative, suggesting that the boundaries that separate spiritual, emotional, or intensely psychological perspectives from a conventional realism are fairly permeable. In these moments, he often uses water imagery that resonates with *Winter Birds* and *My Drowning,* in which Danny and Ellen use river motifs to conceive of the fluidity of time and the mutability and simultaneity of memories and experiences. Watery imagery in *Dream Boy* characterizes both an overwhelming present and the oppression of everyday events weighted by history, a feeling akin to swimming at the bottom of a lake. When the boys first eat lunch together shortly after Nathan arrives at his new school, Nathan examines Roy in the "watery light of the lunchroom," overcome by their paths crossing in this space (7). Later, at Nathan's home, which Paulina Palmer has pointed out conjures the haunting presence of past sexual and emotional abuse, Nathan walks downstairs from his room "as if into some shadowy pool" and "sits underwater and eats," half-remembering past dangers from his father (12).[12] Grimsley also utilizes corresponding descriptions of floating or a radiant nature, as when, during tense dinners with Harland, Nathan's mother appears to be "hovering slightly above the seat of her chair" (45). Analogously, when Nathan and Roy camp together, "Roy's face is . . . luminous from within like flowers at dusk," and both boys feel an ethereal "pulse of happiness" (121). These moments signal not an absence of reality or of wakefulness but a heightened awareness of fear, danger, or natural, spiritual pleasures. They indicate a more complex and thus more uncomfortable or ecstatic understanding of everyday human existence.

Finally, Nathan's ability to hold his own against adversity and the boys' insistence on their loyalty to each other bode well for their future together. While Grimsley gives no assurances, the boys' fortitude, their growing willingness to stand up for themselves, their complex intuition of the infinite potentials of time and space, and their understanding of the interpenetration of pain and pleasure, of life and death all suggest their ability to handle the world that they will head in to, which will be vastly different from any that they have known. This strangeness, moreover, will be countered by their increasing desire to protect each other, to share a partnership, and to give their life together precedence over any other responsibilities and desires, all of which encourages us to anticipate their longevity and happiness as a couple, wherever they go. Wherever they end up, the boys have found a home in each other.

CHAPTER 4

Cities and Suburbs

While Grimsley's early novels focus on a rural or small-town South, he has long maintained an interest in southern cities, particularly those with exotic, grandiose, and often terrifying histories. Never portraying abstract urban landscapes, when Grimsley writes about Atlanta, Savannah, or New Orleans he attends to unique spaces and to monuments, as well as to local legends and customs. Although he acknowledges the increasingly important phenomenon of largely homogeneous suburbs, as in his novel *Forgiveness* (2007), he writes most often about the hearts of cities and their arteries, such as Esplanade Avenue and Royal Street in New Orleans, as in his play *Mr. Universe* (premiered 1987, published 1998) and his novel *Boulevard* (2002). Grimsley demonstrates how these places draw in diverse races, classes, desires, and professions, as long-term residents bring in friends and lovers, forming new family structures, new bonds of kinship that loosen, tighten, or simply force a reassessment of conventional familial relations. Some cities, as Grimsley implies, are more open and welcoming than others, whether by tradition or by necessity, and their economic and social opportunities draw in an eclectic mix of adventure seekers and social outliers who come to find a home, whether a temporary or a permanent one. Although some of these spaces are more inviting than others, even the most prestigious squares of historic Savannah, as we saw briefly with regard to *Comfort and Joy,* turn out to have rigid but not impermeable boundaries, and this is even truer of the less socioeconomically exclusive but still historic urban spaces in which Grimsley tends to linger.

In addition to representing the changing populations of and domestic arrangements in these spaces, Grimsley also demonstrates how streets, buildings, even explanatory placards, so much denser and concentrated in cities than in rural areas, provide a means to explore how myriad historical identities composed of complicated nationalities (such as African, French, Spanish, American), genders (male, female, transgender), sexualities (homosexuality, heterosexuality, pansexuality), and loves, loyalties, and betrayals (of all varieties) can inform and shape the present. Walking through historic districts offers opportunities for sightseeing but also opens up a rich archive for those who can learn to read the appropriate verbal and behavioral natural and architectural signs. Such signs often reveal insights into the past, present, and future of a city and its inhabitants, inspiring reflections on racial cruelty, sexual oppression, religious intolerance, class division, and poverty, as well as on tolerance, respect, a nondogmatic spirituality, and the tarnished triumphs of the sheer will to survive as one's own self. A city, then, can offer a critical cultural education in how the oppressions and freedoms of the past influence contemporary ones. Learning to live in cities helps to distinguish between secondhand and experiential knowledge of the past, as well as between more modern attempts both to survive the past and to transform it. This is true even in contemporary cities overloaded with cheap art, escapist television and film, and advertisements designed to distort any semblance of an ordinary day-to-day life.

Grimsley traces these themes in his characterizations of Atlanta and Savannah in *Comfort and Joy,* and he revisits them in several short stories in his subsequent collection *Jesus Is Sending You This Message* (2008). But Grimsley's interest in cities and suburbs comes to the fore in several works that deserve a closer look, especially those set in New Orleans. After graduating from the University of North Carolina, Grimsley left his home state in 1978 for New Orleans, where he lived for a few years, working in a "liquor store" and taking "phone orders for sanitary maintenance supplies" before moving to Atlanta.[1] These experiences supplied material for two key works set in the outlandish, yet generally welcoming French Quarter, the diversity of which provides a foil for the emotional and psychological isolation of the U.S. suburban wasteland of *Forgiveness* and the unique potentials for community and social alienation provided by the rural circumstances of the Tote-Crell trilogy and *Dream Boy.* This chapter focuses on Grimsley's works concerned with the diametrically opposed settings of New Orleans and an anonymous suburb outside a major, if anonymous, U.S. metropolitan area.

Mr. Universe

First performed in 1987 and restaged frequently thereafter, *Mr. Universe* offers one of Grimsley's most intensive treatments of the sadomasochistic pleasures and pains of an urban locale.[2] Set in 1979 on the edge of New Orleans's French Quarter, Grimsley's play serves up none of the affluence of the Garden District, and there are no southern aristocrats, although several drag queens function as the tarnished, underappreciated royalty of the riverside end of Esplanade. Any refinement, glamour, or fairy-tale happiness in this realm is a flame that flares up quickly before dying away amid the late-night dangers of the Quarter. Indeed, Romulus Linney notes that while the French Quarter "can often seem unreal, a Disneyland of Vice," Grimsley provides us with "the real thing, populated by truthful citizens of its lower depths, those who hustle its streets after hours when tourists are safe in their hotels."[3] Recalling the longing in Tennessee Williams's *Streetcar Named Desire* (1947) and the grittiness of John Rechy's *City of Night* (1963), while adding a surreal streak all his own, Grimsley presents characters who are in various combinations aging drag queens, drugs addicts, and prostitutes.[4] In fact, as Grimsley has noted, the play's "edgy quality" initially derived "partly because of the sexuality of the play, and because drag queens were the *focus* of the action, for a change."[5] This assessment remains true even if one considers Harvey Fierstein's similarly groundbreaking *International Stud,* which premiered in 1978 in New York, providing one of the few drag-queen-focused plays of twentieth-century U.S. theater.

Indeed, in a world that largely de-centers such individuals in reality and in fiction, Grimsley's characters are all strong, alienated individuals trying to make the best home they can, where they can, amid cast-off detritus powerfully symbolic of how society forces aside those who enable its transitory pleasures. The demimonde of the French Quarter, with its strip clubs, bars, and adjacent seedy hotels, offers these individuals some freedom of expression but only a barebones economic subsistence sustained by low-paying, often illegal employment that scarcely supports an apartment, a little food, and drink. Into this already troubled world steps an enigma, a mute Muscle Man who draws the attention of Vick and Judy, two drag queens, in addition to their neighbors Juel Laurie, an elderly, mentally disoriented widow, and Katy Jume, a prostitute. The Muscle Man, a hyperbolic embodiment of a physically virile masculinity, a flesh-and-blood version of Danny Crell's River Man, evokes the potential for romantic and sexual fantasies fulfilled even as, carrying his own trauma, he severely disrupts the lives of those around him. Grimsley uses the Muscle Man's appearance to highlight how, in this harsh, backstabbing world of half-fulfilled pleasures, human kindness and sympathy can thrive against all odds as his characters negotiate for or simply offer to each other support.

From the opening scene, Grimsley elicits sympathy for his social outcasts by refusing to dismiss the worn-out artifacts that litter the streets of so many cities. Indeed, he insists that if one can read the signs of this detritus, it can tell a sympathetic human history. Soon after the curtain opens, Juel Laurie, who variously understands that her husband, Vanice, has died and believes that he lingers on in her apartment, enters the stage to throw out what initially appears to an onstage policewoman to be trash. Yet for Juel Laurie, this trash equates to little domestic jewels, a record of her relationship with Vanice. Holding up one shoe, Juel Laurie declares, "smells just like Vanice," a gesture that evokes further memories of her reminding him to wash his feet. This is a recollection less of nagging or of dirtiness than of everyday domestic intimacies that Juel Laurie longs to remember. Sensing that throwing out Vanice's belongings represents a loss, she hopes to make a list of his items so that she can have a catalogue to remind her of their relationship (8). This list would comfort her, but the move from shoe to a textual catalogued entry of a shoe creates still one more emotional and material remove from Vanice himself. Often, moreover, it proves as difficult to throw out mementos as it does to catalogue them effectively or even to locate what one wants to catalogue. The trash bag Juel Laurie carries from her apartment to the street has a hole in it through which items haphazardly fall out, symbolizing the difficulties both of tossing out memories and of keeping track of them effectively. If we cannot keep every material artifact, a clear impracticality, a record of what we have lost is emotionally and intellectually useful. Still, Grimsley reminds us, any such record will inevitably be incomplete.

Despite this archival incompleteness, Grimsley uses the policewoman in this scene to indicate that public spaces ought not to be overwhelmed with private memories. Reading artifacts takes time, skill, and desire, and for those who have little interest in them, they can become refuse. The policewoman, in other words, tries to make sure that individuals do not dominate public space with their personal histories, even as she remains sensitive to the needs of Juel Laurie. She tells the widow to clean up the mess she has been making, but she does so politely and with respect, calling Juel Laurie "ma'am" (8). Together, moreover, the orderly, officially authoritative policewoman, of whom we know nothing but her public face, and the disorderly Juel Laurie dropping personal items as she crosses the street suggest two counterpointed examples of the performances of femininity available in metropolitan areas.

The conversation between the policewoman and Juel Laurie further suggests how discarded clothes that refigure the city have parallels in unclothed disfigured individuals that similarly offer histories to be interpreted. The policewoman initiates this Kafkaesque correspondence. After telling Juel Laurie to pick up her items, the policewoman reports that a corpse has been found "in a motel over to the Faubourg. . . . Didn't have much of nothing on" (9). The wounds on the man's body indicate a violent death, and his nudity implies sexual violence, imputations that characters guess at throughout the play until they are confirmed by Katy Jume, who admits to having killed the man, leaving his corpse to be cleaned up from the motel. Katy defines the relevant context by characterizing the series of indignities this traveling salesman had inflicted upon her: groping her, inviting her back to his motel room and undressing her, only to demean her further by displaying pictures of his wife, whom Katy recalls has a "nice smile," and then complaining about how his wife doesn't cook his breakfast right, as if to justify his infidelity. Katy recalls growing increasingly disgusted by the man physically and morally, and she explains that when he refused to let her leave, she stabbed him. Frustrated by the man hypocritically vaunting the trappings of lower-middle-class respectability as he simultaneously undermined and degraded these trappings on his spree in the city while Katy lay naked and repulsed before him was too much for her to take. In response, she sought to regain some sense of control, of safety, and of equality, by revenge if necessary: "It felt good to stick a knife up between his ribs. Men always sticking something in me, I wondered how it felt" (53). Consequently, the salesman's messy and rejected body comes to manifest not only his own history of qualified lower-middle-class success, which fuels, financially and psychologically, his covert aggressive escapades in New Orleans but also the trauma of Katy's own life, which has made sex and romance for her cheaply commercial and violent.

The Muscle Man functions as a more peaceful and confused but only slightly less damaged foil to the dead naked salesman, with a history that remains more pointedly mysterious. A Brechtian element incorporated flawlessly into a realistic drama, the mute Muscle Man first appears wandering around as if lost and he subsequently strips down to trunks and covers himself "*with streaks of red paint, like blood, as if he were creating wounds*"; later, "*he paints himself with blood, as before*" (12, 14, 43). D. Bruckner has noted that Grimsley "never gives a clue to the meaning of this symbolism"; yet, while in one sense Bruckner's emphasis on this obscurity is valuable, the character's actions do imply several logical interpretations.[6] The Muscle Man has very likely come to the French Quarter to escape some past trauma, even as the escape remains unfortunately incomplete because he brings his suffering with him, as indicated by the bloodlike paint, a symbol of remembered wounds. "There's something wrong with him," as Vick observes, but the stranger's continued muteness tantalizingly eliminates any certainty as to what that "something wrong" might be beyond his symbolic wounds and his desire to get close to some essential, honest, or revelatory state, a move suggested by his stripping off his clothes (16). Discussing the play, Grimsley has observed that a "certain kind of body obsession," particularly that of a "body builder," "must be linked to self-hatred on some level," and this is likely one wounding element of the Muscle Man's persona.[7] This self-hatred, of course, might be influenced by any number of homophobic, transphobic, or generally queerphobic social mores from which the Muscle Man seeks a qualified safe haven in New Orleans.

Because the stranger either cannot or will not talk, his body must testify to any traumas. They may be psychological, emotional, or spiritual at first, but they eventually affect him materially as his intangible wounds become physical via the paint, which itself hovers between various levels of a symbolic realism. Grimsley describes the Muscle Man painting on his scars first with "*red paint*" and a second time "*with blood,*" a slight yet significant difference in the wording of the stage directions that a live audience could not access but that should complicate readers' understanding of the symbolism of the paint both as a metaphor for blood and as blood. In both cases, nonvisible traumas intensify to become visible through the paint, which the characters treat as real blood from real cuts. Cleaning the Muscle Man, Vick observes that his "cuts aren't all that deep. When they're not bleeding you can hardly see them at all. . . . He's got some bruises too" (21). Whatever the cause of these injuries, Grimsley emphasizes their diverse material and mental effects. The adult man's near physical perfection combined with his inability to articulate, much less to explain, his pain, desires, identity, or memories suggests his infantile or even forcibly stunted intellectual, psychological, and emotional development. The Muscle Man's reapplication of his wounds further suggests their recurring, even self-inflicted nature, perhaps through his preoccupation with them, his inability to forget them much as Juel Laurie cannot forget Vanice or effectively discard his clothes. As such, Vick's observation that the man's "cuts aren't all that deep" opens at least two possibilities. Optimistically, the wounds might heal and leave little permanent damage; pessimistically, any apparent healing into shallower cuts is superficial and transitory, at best, and these wounds will quickly reopen.

Although Grimsley emphasizes the effects of the Muscle Man's wounds, this is not to say that he disregards their implied causes, physical or otherwise. One suggested cause is homophobia, particularly as there are several indications that the Muscle Man is gay. Katy Jume tells Vick that the stranger must be "queer. . . . He a faggot just like you. . . . He got them sweet eyes . . . just like a faggot. He got big faggot muscles. . . . I don't mean to make you mad when I use that word" (23). Katy's contextualization of the slur "faggot" suggests a complex nexus of perceptions: while she associates the slur with positive stereotypes of male homosexuality, such as sweetness, health, and strength, she realizes in the midst of the conversation that the term is offensive, and so she apologizes. This very apology, however, raises the specter of violence and degradation, which Katy wants to avoid and which the Muscle Man may very well have fled from, his flight bringing him to New Orleans. As Scott Ellis has reported, "New Orleans gay life began to blossom more publicly in the 1970s" (the time period directly preceding that of the play), despite some notable backlash.[8] If the Muscle Man is queer, the French Quarter, with its quasi tolerance of homosexuals and other sexual outcasts, would have been a likely place to seek some means to explore his natural same-sex longings and offered a relative refuge from the dangers of homophobia, which still permeated American culture in the late 1970s.

In addition to sexuality, Grimsley also engages anxiety over gender expression as an implied cause of the Muscle Man's and the other characters' personal turmoil. In other words, Grimsley explores what Judith Butler has called performative genders, which coalesce around repeated behaviors and mannerisms that create what only seems to be a prior or an originally innate essence.[9] Since society frequently codes men who act effeminate as gay and gay men as effeminate, much of the discussion regarding the Muscle Man's sexuality stems from questions regarding his performances of masculinity. Upon first seeing the man, Vick notes that he appears "too butch" to be queer, a perspective Vick maintains even after Judy reminds him, "we're not all sissies" (12). When Katy reasserts that the man may be homosexual, Vick more insistently articulates that he does not think the man is gay: "I been spotting faggots for years and I don't think this man is one" (23). Vick, however, inaccurately conflates an explicit effeminacy with homosexuality, and he signals his discomfort with this through his use of the slur "faggot." Vick, in effect, overlooks the stranger's effeminate traits, such as his eyes, his swishy way of standing, and his conventionally feminine care for the body, in order to avoid admitting the man's potential queerness and thereby disrupting his unfortunately self-degrading ideal of a physically fit and masculine heterosexual man. Vick's misguided conflation of effeminacy and homosexuality is, moreover, pointedly ironic, for, despite his penchant for drag, he holds his own effeminacy at a distance, as if uneasy about incorporating it too inextricably into his own life, as if trying to be a noneffeminate gay man and to fulfill at least part of his ideal. In contradistinction to Judy, Vick maintains his given male name, and by Act 1, Scene 2, he has already removed his wig. Vick's lingering insecurities regarding his own quasi-effeminate queerness, which he perceives as an unhappy requirement for entry into publically gay circles, reflects self-destructive conflations of misogyny, effeteness, and queerness. More broadly, it also reflects his fears of appearing too effeminate even in quasi-tolerant urban spaces and his consequent unwillingness to admit the idealized Muscle Man's possible same-sex desires.

Vick's personal insecurities, coupled with his resistance to accepting the Muscle Man's possible queerness, point to how the Muscle Man's dilemma involves his own gender-oriented anxieties. When Judy takes advantage of the Muscle Man's general passivity and puts makeup and a wig on him, he revolts, "*becoming angry*" and agitated (32, 33). As if to reassert a hypernormative masculinity, one predicated on physical strength, he "*flexes his arms as if proving his manhood . . . almost in a frenzy*" (33). This posing frenzy signals a frustrated self-doubt. Yet, unlike with Vick, the stranger objects not simply to drag or to feminine attributes but also to having them forced on him by an external agent, for he later tries on the wig of his own accord and smiles (37). The Muscle Man is willing to experiment with gender performance and to interrogate his self-doubt in a way that makes him happy, but only on his own terms, when he feels safe.

Vick, Judy, and their associates in the French Quarter provide the Muscle Man with a model and, at times, a relatively safe space to test the positive potentials of drag. For despite Vick's trepidations and Judy's aggression, Grimsley evokes the qualified power of drag when used as a means to reaffirm one's identity. Judy reminds Vick that not all gay men are sissies, but Grimsley implies that sissiness can lead to a sassiness that creates both glamour in a sordid environment and, more important, moral fortitude.[10] Judy and Vick insist on their splendor by carefully putting on lipstick, wigs, even alligator pumps, and they are certainly nobler in their honest pursuit of their own identities than the "straight" men who hide "weddings ring[s]" to court queens in queer bars and then attack the queens who discover their infidelities, as has happened with Judy (20). Judy and Vick might at times delude themselves regarding their happiness and strength, as evidenced by their encounter with the "straight" man whom Judy initially mocks and who subsequently attacks her and Vick and ruins their evening. They pursue, nonetheless, an honest identity and deserve more respect than the middle-aged men who persist in publicly denying their sexuality while betraying their wives by picking up other men in dark bars. In this world, the drag queens hold the moral high ground, if not much political power.

As if to fortify this morality, Grimsley shows these characters using their shared acceptance of taboo yet harmless desires to form a tightly knit community structured according to reimagined kinship bonds. Judy mockingly refers to Vick as "the Mother Superior of Esplanade," but Vick does take on a valuable quasi-maternal role for several outcast characters (34). He has taken in Judy, her biological family having abandoned her, and he gives Katy a place to hide while the police look for her in connection with the murder in the Faubourg. Having found the Muscle Man on the street, Vick shelters and cleans him up, not for self-centered sexual purposes but to give him someplace safe to stay. This is a potentially educational moment, since the stranger seems primarily to understand interpersonal relationships in terms of physical interactions. As Vick dresses his wounds, he flexes his muscles, posing, only to have Vick respond, "they're real pretty. . . . But I don't need a show right now" (45). To the Muscle Man's initial confusion, Vick avoids a physical erotic connection and focuses on nursing him. In fact, he almost always touches the Muscle Man solely to dress his wounds. Vick thereby exemplifies how sexual attraction can coexist with, yet be subordinate to, other forms of positive attention. Katy Jume reinforces such nurturing relationships. After she realizes that the Muscle Man lacks interest in her, she encourages his attraction to Vick and takes the blame when it appears, incorrectly, that the Muscle Man has murdered Judy so as to give him and Vick a chance to find happiness together. To a less intense degree, Juel Laurie helps Vick and Katy by warning them that the police are looking for Katy. "You got to treat your neighbors like your kin," she explains (49). Geographically and psychically distanced from traditional families and thrown into close quarters with neighbors because of the constraints of poverty and a crowded city, these characters demonstrate the benefits of reimagining familial roles to create a flexible support system.

While the diverse, crowded, occasionally tolerant city can facilitate new sympathetic kinships, *Mr. Universe* acknowledges how dangers nonetheless exist because of the potential for anonymous violence with minimal risk of retribution. Even in the case of known aggressors, real-life New Orleans judicial agents as recently as the 1960s and early 1970s showed little interest in rebuking those who assaulted or murdered queer or allegedly queer individuals, thereby signaling official permission to commit aggression toward these citizens.[11] Thus Vick refuses to walk along the waterfront with Judy to look for sailors because he fears that they might get killed by some homophobic man passing through town (11). Judy knows better than to go to the river by herself, especially when she remains scared to walk alone on Esplanade in drag at night. Tourists and residents of the French Quarter may be more tolerant of the nontraditional genders and sexualities ghettoized in that space, but this tolerance is predicated upon a ghettoization that provides a freer because curtailed and largely unseen expression of identities and libidos. New Orleans's tolerance is thus qualified, and Grimsley's characters know better than to rely entirely on the kindness of strangers. Strangers assault Vick, Judy, and Katy in bars that they had thought were welcoming, and Katy's interaction with the antagonistic traveling salesman in the Faubourg motel room emphasizes the potential for rape and murder, even if murder in self-defense. These incidents evoke the dangers inherent in an urban culture that only loosely accepts nonnormative desires. It also evokes the danger when this very curtailed acceptance attracts transient individuals who seek the commodification of exciting taboo sex or the promise thereof, which remains much less readily available in other, more rural areas. This space where sex is so easily bought and sold and where drag queens, queers, and sex workers are largely disenfranchised offers not only the promise of pleasure but also the potential for violent or transient individuals to escape the emotional, ethical, and even legal consequences of their actions.

These realities pose external dangers to reimagined extended family structures. Grimsley focuses most extensively, however, on the internal dangers that erupt when the opportunities provided by even an urban area are not enough to relieve social pressures and their consequent strains. Grimsley shows this process most extensively through Judy. Although 1979-era New Orleans offered more options to queer individuals than many other American spaces, the ghettoization and stigmatization of dissident sexualities limited even these, and in *Mr. Universe* Judy grows increasingly frustrated by such restraints and indignities. Walking along Esplanade, she laments, "I am not interested in one bar up that street," referring to Bourbon Street (11). Then, when Vick somewhat unfairly criticizes Judy for getting into her fight with the married man at the bar where they do end up, he aggravates her already infuriated state and she half-mockingly and half-seriously threatens to kill Vick, saying, "if I had a gun I'd blow your brains out right here" (15). Judy's hostility adds an uncomfortably intimate layer of danger to the danger presented by strangers, one that takes on an insidious subtlety as Grimsley shows Judy manipulatively dealing drugs in Vick's apartment. Calling Katy "sister" and sweet-talking her, Judy gives Katy "crystal" (methamphetamine) in an attempt to convince Katy to help her have sex with the Muscle Man without Vick's knowledge, and subsequently Judy arranges for the police to discover that Katy is staying at Vick's apartment (42, 44). These acts constitute betrayals on several levels, including Judy's facilitation of Katy's drug addiction, her faithless exploitation of a sisterly relationship to get Katy arrested, and her encouraging Katy to be disloyal to Vick. More insidious, she attempts to disrupt Vick's burgeoning connection with the stranger and threatens Vick's freedom and his tenancy of his apartment by storing drugs in it.

Judy's final treachery occurs when she attempts to murder one of the group and ends up destroying herself, suggesting the self-harm that can come from viciously attacking one's community. After the Muscle Man rejects Judy's advances, she attempts to stab him in revenge. He resists, and in the ensuing struggle the knife turns and she causes her own accidental death. With a bittersweet irony, the struggle "*ends in an embrace,*" an isolated death replacing the longed-for *petite mort* of an orgasm with another person (61). Judy's combined anger at the world and her willingness to turn against the people who nurture or associate with her create the greatest immediate menace to her small circle and to herself.

One of *Mr. Universe*'s great tragedies is nonetheless Judy's self-destruction through her uncritical pursuit of personal pleasure and her lack of interest in the needs of others as she seeks to wrest some romance from her world. Judy initially pursues the Muscle Man, for instance, to satisfy her own physical and psychological longings rather than to enter into a relationship, no matter how brief. When Vick observes that there is something wrong with the stranger, Judy replies, "not from where I'm standing," and, regarding the stranger's muteness, she comments, "that's fine with me, he'll never need to say a word" (16). Judy offers an inherently selfish reaction to the Muscle Man, lusting after his physical appeal only, desiring no intellectual intercourse with him, and giving no thought to his obvious problems. She insists, "I'm not interested in his identity problems," only "his social life," and when she says "social" she clearly means sexual (34). Still, Grimsley portrays Judy's self-centeredness with remarkable sympathy, characterizing it as a defensive counterbalance to a world that for years has undermined her search for love and admiration. Amid pursuing the all-too-passive Muscle Man, Judy finally breaks down: "I've done this before, I'm sick of it. You can't just stand there, you can't just wait. You have to come to me. You have to want me too" (59). With this cri de cœur Judy resembles both Tennessee Williams's delusional, romantically thwarted heroines and Lillian Hellman's quietly ferocious Regina Hubbard, who, after years of submitting to the men in her family, insists at the end of *The Little Foxes,* "somewhere there has to be what I want, too."[12] Hubbard sacrifices others to gain sufficient money to win her independence, material luxuries, and power over others; analogously, Judy sacrifices sympathy to win erotic attention and, on a basic level, someone to desire her openly. As such, she tries to force sex or romance by urging the Muscle Man to respond to her unreciprocated desires. In doing so, she lashes out against men who satisfy their lusts by submitting passively to her attentions, while hiding their desire for her and ruining any chance at romance in an attempt not to compromise their normative, socially acceptable masculinity.

In desperation, Judy finally evolves by reaching back toward a desire for mutual understanding, but Grimsley portrays her as too tragically flawed by anger and egotism to find happiness, toward which Vick and the Muscle Man inch through their sustained vital sympathy. Trying to get the Muscle Man into bed, Judy begs, "if you would just let me try I could be okay. . . . You don't have to pretend anymore. This is what you came here for, isn't it?" (59). Judy is undoubtedly right: the Muscle Man came to New Orleans and, more specifically, to Vick's apartment to stop pretending and to figure out both who he is and who he wants to be, to experiment with nonnormative freedoms, genders, and sexualities, as well as new social structures. But Grimsley implies through his characters' divergent fates that to try fleetingly to be okay, to try to understand individuals in order to inspire their erotic attraction, is not enough, and Judy's attempt at mutual intimacy quickly reverts to the aggression that ends her life. Vick, Grimsley indicates, survives because he balances caring for the physical with an attempt to learn about and to care for others. Using a pragmatic strategy of delayed gratification that will benefit himself and those around him, Vick tries to discover the stranger's past in order to better orient their possible future together, not simply for sex but for a mature, interactive relationship. Acting analogously to Vick, in the final scene of the play the Muscle Man reaches down to feel Judy's fatal wound and then "*smears the red on himself, as before*" (66). The effect may be the same "*as before,*" but its connotations have evolved significantly. The stranger's gesture reinforces his attraction to danger and aggression. It also, however, suggests that the body builder identifies sympathetically with the pain and self-destructive behavior caused by Judy's social isolation and her myopic self-importance and that he is working, if now too late, to understand her.

The Muscle Man performs this gesture privately—only the audience sees it—which both echoes his earlier private experimentations with the wig and suggests that he can transcend his narcissism to a degree impossible for Judy, as his sympathy is not a public form of showing off. Accordingly, even though the Muscle Man has only ever communicated his attraction to Vick by staying close to him and though he responds to Vick's final question, "what am I going to do with you?," only by facing him, Grimsley offers hope that whatever happens between them, it will be a well-intentioned, mutual endeavor (66). As Gary Richards has convincingly noted, Grimsley's play thereby revises Williams's trajectory in *A Streetcar Named Desire,* in which Blanche's reliance on "the kindness of strangers" eventually "leads to rape, abandonment, and institutionalization," by having his Muscle Man's encounter with Vick, in particular, bring an "escape from tragedy and derision, even if the ultimate result is left ambiguous."[13] In this way, his having the Muscle Man and Vick face each other leads to an ambiguous ending, to be sure, yet one that is cautiously optimistic. Grimsley's ending to *Mr. Universe* depicts a universal uncertainty that forces us to pose to make ourselves more acceptable even as we frequently fail to articulate our own desires accurately, both to ourselves and to others; it predominantly evokes an almost universally relatable longing to care for and to be cared for by others.

Boulevard

In *Boulevard,* Grimsley's exploration into private and public desires evolves by returning to the setting of New Orleans. He does so to emphasize how cities, particularly those with long historical trajectories, can intertwine uniquely personal and communal educations that substantially affect the desires of those individuals who live in them. With greater breadth than in *Mr. Universe,* Grimsley traces in *Boulevard* the connections and parallels between the social and racial oppressions of the past and the sexual oppressions that existed at the time the novel's events took place, in 1976, as well as at the time of its publication, in 2002. Beginning with the classic provincial-boy-moves-to-the-big-city motif, Grimsley has his young protagonist, Newell, leave his limited Alabama town for the cultural, racial, and sexual opportunities that were burgeoning in New Orleans in the mid-1970s but which had still not obtained widespread acceptance almost thirty years later, an irony that Grimsley's novel implicitly highlights.[14] Grimsley quickly complicates this conventional motif by representing the various educational opportunities available in an urban area as Newell discovers how a complex city can rework itself economically and socially over centuries to expand its heritage.

Analogously to how Grimsley showed Juel Laurie interpreting refuse on the street, he tracks Newell's penchant for reading the city in an increasingly complex fashion. Newell quickly graduates from examining a map to perusing newspapers, historical plaques, a guide book, and stories about the French Quarter, and buildings themselves (3, 5, 6, 48, 113). This is an experiential, immersive form of learning, emotive, practical, and intellectual, and Newell quickly intuits how the socioeconomic and racial cruelties of the past linger insidiously in the present, where they get reworked with ambivalent results. Soon after arriving, he walks down a street and observes "buildings, fences, and gates, and he had the feeling that all this was to hide what went on inside these buildings. . . . Over the tops of fences he could see the backs of houses, many with smaller buildings running perpendicular to the back. These must be what were called slave quarters—he'd seen a slave quarter apartment described that way in the classifieds" (19–20). The city, he realizes, was built upon a series of exclusionary forces, jointly architectural and social, that civic elites wanted both to vaunt and to conceal, revealing the system of mastery and slavery yet hiding the brutality that it enabled. Relatively affluent and influential twentieth-century families subsequently muted the vicious cruelties of slavery into exponentially less sadistic forms of commodifiable spatial divisions. Renovated slave quarters now advertised as living quarters for those with moderately low incomes advantageously signal a progression beyond slavery and provide decent rooms in the Quarter for people such as Newell. Yet, these apartments ambiguously reinforce socioeconomic borders while simultaneously concealing a horrifically racist and classist history.

Indeed, Newell senses that reasons for secrecy here may have shifted only to cover subtler economic and sexual indignities. In an old copy of George Washington Cable's *Strange True Stories of Louisiana* (1890), purchased from his landlady, Louise, Newell reads of aristocrats exiled after the French Revolution, of the U.S. Civil War, and, most horrifically, of Delphine Lalaurie. Lalaurie tortured the enslaved individuals in her house so horrendously that one girl leaped to her death and an old woman set fire to the Lalaurie mansion to escape being chained to the kitchen. Setting the book down, Newell walks to "the back gallery" of the room he rents in a house not far from the Lalaurie mansion and "looked at the slave quarters, which Louise had fixed up into such a nice apartment for herself" (115). Louise's remodeling of her property has allowed her to run a junk store, a business symbolic of repurposing the past rather than obsessing over it; to rent out a room to earn extra money; and to live quietly in the Quarter—all of which represent a problematically positive revitalizing of buildings with sickening associations. If it is unhealthy to obsess over the past, it is equally dangerous to plaster it over and forget its lessons or to commodify it uncritically, as Louise does. For Newell discerns uncomfortable ghostly resemblances between racial and sexual abuse as Louise uses the privacy afforded by her walls and fences to conduct an affair with an increasingly unwilling young girl on the edge of puberty, whom she employs in her shop. While Grimsley rightly avoids simplistic conflations of racial and sexual abuse or of enslavement and employment, through his use of setting he suggests faint yet real correspondences between them that deserve recognition, if only to prevent slippages toward increased exploitation and oppression in the future.

Part of the difficulty in untangling these correspondences, in halting any system of abuse, and in narrowing unjust socioeconomic divisions, Grimsley suggests, is that they stem from an entrenched web of racial, legal, economic, and aesthetic precedents. Newell recognizes this web in its most public manifestations as he idles alongside famous edifices, reading their "historical plaques," "learning about the Cabildo, the Spanish colonial administration, the Pontalba buildings" (25). The Cabildo has housed Spanish, French, and American government representatives, as well as the Louisiana State Supreme Court and, since 1911, collections from the Louisiana State Museum.[15] The Upper and Lower Pontalba buildings were built in the mid–nineteenth century for Micaela Almonester, the Baroness de Pontalba, with stores on the ground level and apartments above, and have been owned by the city and by the Louisiana State Museum since 1930 and 1926, respectively.[16] Consequently, coexisting with the beautiful, fascinating, and dazzlingly diverse multiracial and multicultural influences of the African, Spanish, and French occupants of the Quarter and their descendants are reminders of still influential brutal colonial interventions. These buildings emphasize how the interwoven public and personal socioeconomic hierarchies of New Orleans have molded and continue to mold the modern Quarter. Yet, this selfsame evolving continuity, built upon a reputation for excess, decadence, and cruelty, gradually fostered multicultural attractions and social and sexual freedom, if not necessarily political tolerance. This multifaceted economy accordingly supports the myriad stores selling anything from antiques to pornography, the cafés with their po'boys and beignets, and the bars and clubs catering to a continuum of genteel drinkers and drugged-out dancers that draw Newell, and so many like him, to New Orleans as a place to explore a more cosmopolitanism aesthetic than that offered in small towns and to discover and refine their own individual tastes and characters.

Through Mark Duval, an amateur historian from an old, affluent New Orleans family, Grimsley portrays the dangers of fixating on the horrors and fascinating decadence of this past. Unlike Louise, who converts old tragedies into new life even as she echoes old socioeconomic injustices enabled by class and age hierarchies, Mark obsesses about uncovering his family's crimes against humanity and remembering them in the present. Having listened to family legends while younger and having "studied history" and philosophy, specifically Nietzsche, at Tulane, Mark delves into his family's long association with the sadism that aristocratic wealth and privilege can facilitate. Mark considers and studies his family's past—from an ancestor's chance encounter with the Marquis de Sade, a symbol of the pitiless aristocratic excesses countered by the French Revolution, to the Duval family's acquisition, in nineteenth-century New Orleans, of property, opium, and enslaved individuals, including biological children who were owned "as slaves" (Grimsley's critique of certain traditional family structures in the United States)—only to have this past overwhelm his present (193). With the leisure to linger over yellowing family archives and to explore the psychological aftereffects of his ancestry through drugs, Mark exists as an enervated embodiment of his family's intoxicating perversion of Nietzsche's Will to Power into a Will to Profligacy. Tripping on LSD, Mark "see[s] ghosts" throughout the city and "echoes of past houses that have burned down or fallen down or been torn down," apparitions that he becomes convinced are real (191–92). Mark's present-day decadence, his attempts to understand his ancestors by emulating their pursuit of power, drugs, and sex, leads to his own debilitation. Mark's grasp on reality becomes tenuous, and, despite his privileges and in a wonderfully subtle echo of the mute Muscle Man, he cannot articulate his own accounts of himself. Talking to Newell soon after they meet, Mark gets confused, and his "story itself dissolve[s]" (187). Mark's historical obsessions themselves become intoxicating, as much as the drugs he takes, so that his life, like the dilapidated buildings he envisions, is an exhausted and exhausting mess.

As Grimsley indicates, Mark's dilemma stems largely from his use of his heritage to facilitate his personal decadence, which creates his conscious complicity in the practice of social and racial violence from the French Revolution through American slavery to present-day economic disparities. To relieve his guilt, he consistently disrupts any present pleasure with self-punishing and yet concurrently self-promoting recollections of this traumatic past, reminding himself of his family's crimes and power. In bed with Newell, for instance, as Mark thinks about his ancestors, he asks Newell to slap him (187). Subsequently, when Newell fellates him, Mark thinks of a slaveholding relative's memoir of riots incited by Delphine Lalaurie's cruelty: "in the Bourbon Pub, he was thinking about the existence of the self . . . that he could alter it and yet remain, or even become more intensely, a construction. . . . Getting a blow job . . . on acid . . . and Mark himself bemused at the thought of history. A perfect moment in the search for the good and the beautiful" (216). Grimsley's skillful interweaving of Mark's fascination with the trauma revealed by his research, recalled during his sexual experiences with Newell, suggests that Mark's search has less to do with "the good and the beautiful" than with his construction of a heavily flawed poetic justice, a masochistic atonement for his existence that is also an oblivion. This bittersweet search for oblivion will intensify later when he switches from acid to heroin.

Mark's search leaves him in ironic isolation at a time when he should be enjoying his safe sexual encounters as homosexuality becomes more accepted, although still decades away from being legal, and with the threat of HIV/AIDS still unknown. Yet, rather than focus on ecstatically overcoming existing barriers or performing socially useful tasks such as teaching or writing up his research, he instead experiments with tempering pleasure with pain. These experiments serve, paradoxically, as penance for his profit from and pride in tyrannical power and as a means to find a destructively pleasurable stupefaction. Consequently, Mark exemplifies corresponding characters in the novel such as the masochistic owner of the adult bookstore where Newell works, the owner's sadistic nephew, Jack, and Mark's distant relative Leigh, a debauched aristocratic debutante.

If Grimsley uses these characters to signal how lingering obsessions with urban ghosts can "Mark" or scar one's psyche and body, then Newell exemplifies a "Newe[r]" or fresher approach to the city that more equitably balances the past with the present to enhance a personal maturation. Newell, accordingly, learns from the chronological continuum of New Orleans to develop his own intellectual and sexual identity. In addition to reading historical markers and literature, Newell attends to the living environment around him, as when he notices "a man who was pretending to be a woman and making money for it," which he interprets as "a clear sign that the world was larger than anything [he] could ever have learned about in Pastel," Alabama (28). As he advances in techniques for interpreting New Orleans' architecture, he follows a similar path with his sexual evolution, moving from general speculation of what naked men look like to knowledge acquired through pornographic magazines and movies to a more experiential education via voyeurism and participation in the erotic atmosphere of bars, the riverfront, private apartments, and work as a clerk in a porn store that tangentially functions as a sex club (53). For Newell, the city becomes a site for (homo)sexual initiation rather than for colonial conquest, as the stimulating move from lackluster Pastel to the neon of New Orleans prepares him for an intoxicating because evolving engagement with the multi-faceted nature of U.S. culture. After smoking pot on his first evening of sexual voyeurism, Newell considers that the "drug had altered his perception of the world" even as "the world he was coming to know was itself a narcotic" (104). Unlike Mark's enervating drug abuse, Newell's moderate experiments with mind-altering substances runs parallel to his experience with the populace of the city, where he sees men with "every color of skin, every texture," allowing him to find friendships, romantic relationships, a sense of "ecstasy . . . like a window opening," and "the feeling of a tribe around him" (100, 106). Newell discovers freedom and opportunities, and as a result he feels like an "adult and in control of the world" (110). In contrast to Mark's drugged oblivion, Newell's mind-expanding encounters encourage him to engage a variety of genders, sexualities, races, and social classes, and this gives him a healthy, if slightly overinflated, sense of belonging and self-determination.

While Mark sneers at Newell's allegedly provincial approach to the world, Grimsley presents it as leading to valuable self-control through self-knowledge regarding personal distinctions between pleasure and pain and a life-affirming rejection of self-harm. As Newell advances his self-discovery through his immersion in public New Orleans culture, he increasingly pursues bondage and rough sex, yet this pursuit differs from Mark's self-destructive masochism, and it tellingly culminates in the final section, "Reason to Live." After an evening of extreme sex with Jack that veers into violence—"sex that had turned into a beating"—Newell discovers his unpreparedness for this level of physical and psychic intensity (291). Simultaneously, he realizes that his continued eroticization of Jack harmfully conflates pleasure and pain and warps the boundaries of consent. To what degree, he wonders, will acquiescence to his desire for Jack be mingled with reluctance? Consequently, he flees Jack because of his "fear of what it meant to say yes" (290). Newell's desire to "say yes" is itself troublingly ambiguous. Perhaps Jack correctly surmises that Newell's ambivalent consent aids a quest to "*mak[e] sense of things a moment at a time,*" a quest for knowledge through distinctions that itself provides a "*reason to survive*" (287). One longs to survive, Grimsley suggests, in order to know one's self completely, which can be achieved by exploring both how sensations vary according to time, place, motivations and one's own evolving responses.

Jack's interpretation, however, as Grimsley makes clear, may be valid, but it is only partial because Jack views Newell through the distancing paradigm of movie-going. While with Newell, Jack reflects that "*it is like a movie to watch him, a silvered image, a surface*" (287). Movies, as Grimsley indicates throughout Newell's bildungsroman-like trajectory, afford a useful heuristic device for discovery, but they are ultimately incomplete, providing a superficial surface, an imaginary representation that emphasizes a glimmering ideal.[17] With a greater sense of interiority, Newell realizes that the nature of consent is a slippery slope, changing according to situation and time, and that his own initial consent might harm him. Unlike Mark, he has the mental fortitude to stop himself before he pushes beyond what he can cope with in in a given moment. Accordingly, he leaves New Orleans so that his excitement and desire will not overcome him, causing him to return to Jack.

On a formal level, we might note that Grimsley frequently juxtaposes individuals' private sexual encounters with descriptions of public cultural conditions, as we have seen with Mark's experience in the Bourbon Pub. As such, it is worth considering how Newell's rejection of Jack interacts with the novel's concern with a liberalizing social progress and with historical guilt. Despite Newell's ambivalence regarding the relationship between sex and violence, his exit from New Orleans can be read as a rejection of excessive sadomasochism as too dangerous despite its being, at times, enticing, erotic, and, as he saw through Mark, a possible expiation of and relief from historical culpability. In a way, Newell's rejection of Mark and Jack allows him a chance to advance to his own social maturity. "There were so many other places to live, now that he had lived in New Orleans," Newell thinks as he returns to Alabama to recover before capitalizing on the self-empowerment he has gained in New Orleans (292). Newell's direct engagement with his own past in Alabama is telling with regard to this self-empowerment. He keeps in touch with small-town Alabama throughout the novel, largely through Grimsley's clever use of Newell's conscientious yet short phone calls to his grandmother, but he never lets this past consume him, despite the offensive homophobic language he encounters, such as his grandmother's calling her boyfriend a sissy for smoking cigarillos, which she calls "faggot sticks" (269, 270). Newell's ability to engage his history and to transcend it suggests that he has taken responsibility for and control over his own present and has the ability to move forward. Clearly, Newell's personal history correlates only *very* loosely with the much more complex engagements of New Orleans and the United States with past and present racial, gendered, and economic injustices. Yet, Grimsley subtly suggests here that society at large must find a way to attend to and compensate for these traumas through new economic and psychological strategies without becoming impotently engulfed by them.

Grimsley bolsters this suggestion by paralleling and even surpassing Newell's will for survival in the character Miss Sophia, an older male-born woman. While Miss Sophia might be considered trans, it is best to resist this descriptor partly because she never refers to herself as such and partly because, as David Valentine has argued with regard to trans identities, "the goals and logics of identity politics themselves" can produce an "apparent unintelligibility and erase an analysis of the entrenched inequalities that underpin them," thereby distracting from unique struggles toward self-definition.[18] Miss Sophia represents the novel's most powerful embodiment of someone who has positively evolved from her past toward a unique self-definition, only to encounter significant pushback from the world around her.[19] Miss Sophia's precise history is unclear, in part because of her having so drastically distanced herself from it, a distance that in itself indicates her successful solidification of her womanhood. This success is nonetheless qualified, for traces of her lingering past hint at what she has lost in her evolution or transition from man to woman. Recounting Miss Sophia's mental wanderings, Grimsley implies that she was once a "fine attorney from an old New Orleans family" with an "office on Gravier" in the neoclassical "Whitney Building" (155). Having gained the freedom to pursue her femininity by rejecting the authority of overtly manmade laws and customs, illustrated by her quitting her legal practice, Miss Sophia loses intellectually, financially, and socially, as this once "fine attorney" takes a job cleaning the adult bookstore where Newell works and as she now lives in a small apartment on the pleasant but not quite upscale South Bunny Friend Street. She learns to enjoy and to take pride in her work, but Grimsley rightfully recalls here the difficulties and indignities suffered by many intelligent, capable individuals like Miss Sophia whose employment and living options decrease because of other people's prejudices and their own concerns for safety.

While Miss Sophia might not be an ideal role model for a modern trans community, and undoubtedly Grimsley never attempts to make her one, he explicitly imbues her with a spectacular resiliency as she adheres to her simultaneously natural and constructed identity. If Miss Sophia longs occasionally to be one of the prettiest boys in the Quarter—a reminder of the too often internalized male-centered normatives that plague the queer community, as much as any other—she feels generally comfortable with her instinctive femininity. Even in the midst of costuming herself for churchgoing, for which she dresses in a suit, she retains her womanhood: "it was amazing even to her" to see herself looking like a man, and "it never occurred to her to question the logic of this, that she, a woman, should dress in clothing of the opposite sex in order to go to church"

(155). For her, to dress like a man is cross-dressing, and for the church to insist, implicitly or otherwise, that she do this is a perversion and against her nature, even if she never questions it. Yet, for the majority of the week, she directs her own life by self-identifying and wearing clothes that reflect her individual normality and value: she perceives herself variously as "only an ordinary person" and as someone who has created and embodied a valuable self, for she "had invented Miss Sophia . . . and she was far more interesting to inhabit than nearly anybody" (154, 153). Accordingly, with Miss Sophia, Grimsley empathically illustrates both the difficulties regarding gender presentation, particularly for some individuals, and a difficult but certainly effective example of self-acceptance through self-fulfillment, a twist on the American dream of the self-made man.

To honor such achievements, Grimsley emphasizes Miss Sophia's power of self-control and her moral responsibility. When deep despondency and a resulting craving for alcohol occasionally plague her, Grimsley describes how she keeps working and moving by "force of will" and resists drinking completely to keep from harming herself (161). Her will proves exponentially stronger than that of anyone else in the novel, including Newell, who, being a young, beautiful, cisgender male, has significantly fewer social pressures. Grimsley makes clear that it is Miss Sophia's acceptance of her own unconventional identity, her self-disciplined refusal to revert regularly to a facade of masculinity or to drink, two analogous forms of escapism, that allows her to triumph over her pain and her culturally induced depression. This will to a firm identity, furthermore, connects intrinsically to her sense of the moral responsibility of ordering one's life. "Anonymity produces pigdom," she thinks, because "when nobody is looking, we are apt to do anything, make any kind of mess, and leave it for others to attend to." Rather than lapse into "pigdom," Miss Sophia realizes that no one will take care of her, not respectfully, so she takes responsibility for herself. She "kept her house immaculately clean," Grimsley tells us, and this is an analogy for her keeping her mind and conscience as clear as she can so as not to make a mess for others to resolve (154). This process allows Miss Sophia to sustain what composure and happiness she can in her social and financial position. To validate Miss Sophia's moral fortitude, and to emphasize the importance of such gender-nonconformist individuals to the queer experience, Grimsley gives Miss Sophia the last scene of the novel as he shows her watching Newell leave New Orleans and then returning to her clean home in the city to have coffee and king cake, a largely, if not entirely, satisfied woman.

Forgiveness

After *Boulevard,* Grimsley turned, in his novel *Forgiveness,* from the exoticism of New Orleans, a nationally renowned southern city, to its degraded cousin, an anonymous and ostensibly affluent suburban wasteland. Using this wasteland as a background, Grimsley depicts the downfall of the Stranger family to provide a biting and at times quite funny satire of the *nouveau riche* upper middle class in the United States in the wake of the 2001–2002 Enron scandal, a formal and thematic shift for Grimsley and further evidence of his literary versatility. Grimsley details how the Strangers' alienation from one another and from U.S. society stems from their individual refusal to examine the consequences of their greed and their self-centeredness aside from the immediate discomfort that they experience when Charles Stranger loses his prestigious job at Arthur Andersen. Such myopia, Grimsley argues, sets off a chain reaction resulting in severe psychological distress and, eventually, physical harm. As such, Grimsley uses the Strangers to demonstrate how the violence and the alienation that characterize the commercial excessiveness of a large part of the U.S. economy, motivated by avarice, selfishness, and a desire for unsustainable luxury, can reflect destructively not just the country at large but also the personal lives of those whom it supposedly benefits.

Grimsley weaves descriptions of this violence into passages written in a style that might be called "commercial surrealism," a term that signals not a cheap or a poorly done avant-garde but rather a style that parodies the dreamlike rhetoric of television commercials designed to capitalize on middle-class consumers' impractical acquisitiveness and the violent absurdities promoted and validated by talk shows that market themselves to voyeuristic audiences frustrated with their own lives. While in *Boulevard,* Grimsley linked a cinematic view of the world with late twentieth-century juvenile perspectives, in *Forgiveness* he extends this critique by mapping symbiotic connections among irresponsibility, violence, alienation, and the frantic celebrity worship encouraged by a prurient modern media. More specifically, he fashions his new foray into satirizing the suburban upper middle class to critique the math (literally and metaphorically) and aftermath of avaricious commercial practices and the self-righteous, myopic self-absorption that facilitated the American financial scandals at the turn of the twenty-first century, as well as the hypocrisy of society's conservative, heterosexist privileging of the traditional nuclear family.[20] In *Forgiveness,* then, Grimsley critiques "pigdom," to borrow Miss Sophia's term, on a presentist scale unimagined in the previous novels.

Grimsley caricatures the hypocrisy, the irresponsibility, and ultimately the psychological laziness of corrupt American businesspeople through Charles "Charley" Ebenezer Stranger. An unrepentant inversion both of Ebenezer Scrooge from Charles Dickens's *A Christmas Carol* and of Meursault from Albert Camus's *The Stranger,* Charley spends lavishly on the rapidly depreciating luxuries of his upper-middle-class American lifestyle, which he commits to by continuing to buy into it, quite literally, even after he has lost his job at Arthur Andersen following the accounting firm's collapse, in 2002.[21] Initially unable to confess his unemployment to his wife, Carmine, who herself never questions where their money comes from, Charley buys "new golf clubs," "a new riding lawn mower," and a "more expensive slip" for his boat, while tolerating his willfully uninformed wife's decision to "redo the kitchen" and to "buy new furniture for the guest house" of their suburban mansion (43, 44). In part this spending allows Charley to try to perceive himself as the virile heterosexual alpha male epitomized in advertisement-saturated urban and suburban landscapes. His purchases allow him to be part of the society promoted by a television vehicle commercial wherein a "perfect" wife and her powerful husband drive their SUV up the side of a Manhattan skyscraper, a surrealistic image of consumerism promising unrealistic attainments (2). Just as living in an expensive, exclusive suburb isolates Charley from drastically different social classes and prevents him from having to consider American poverty, spending on credit and even the fantasy of spending on credit keep him from having to assess honestly his untenable upper-middle-class status.

This commercialized bubble also distracts from the pitfalls of what Grimsley presents as a market economy of emotions. Spending allows Charley to keep the superficial peace of his family's unsympathetic coexistence. As he puts it, "it always comes down to some kind of purchase, to some exchange involving the market. We hurt one another in some way . . . and in response we buy something." Money and a desire for luxuries provide a plaster that covers deeper structural cracks and a diversion that keeps one from contemplating or fixing them. The problem with this, Grimsley suggests, is that relying on money as an easy fix rather than trying to understand or to sympathize with family members, particularly spouses, leads to isolation within the community. As Charley realizes, in his marriage "there had never been any question of pulling together to do anything; the money had done everything for us, there had never been any reason to make much of an effort" (51). For the Strangers, who may have originally been kind to each other, financial power leads to the atrophy of the will to work as a team and to communicate in a mutually beneficial fashion.

Part of this greed and emotional laziness, Grimsley argues, stems from the gendered norms of modern middle- and upper-class America, to which Grimsley suggests that the Strangers cave somewhat consciously, to their detriment. Once, in a fleeting moment of critical reflection, Charley recollects being young and telling Carmine not to work: "I was in a state of shock. I had just told Carmine . . . to quit her job, and even though I had clearly said the words of my own volition I wasn't quite sure why" (47). The cause of the shock and the reason why stem from Charley's unexpected conformity to ill-conceived notions of affluent masculinity that dictate that the husband support a demure, homemaking wife. Despite wondering, briefly, whether abandoning her job means the sacrifice of her loyalty to "women's lib," a loyalty that proves all too easily disowned, Carmine agrees to Charley's request, saying, "you're so good to me, Charley" (47, 48). Charley filters Carmine's eagerness to sacrifice her feminist independence for a life of leisure through his resentment, overlooking the fact that he told rather than asked her to stop working, but the effects of their ultimately joint decision to follow normative gendered work patterns are nonetheless disastrous. Carmine has long had the luxury of not having to consider the way the economy works, and this ignorance contributes to their financial debacle. For example, even after she discovers Charley's unemployment, she persists in spending money excessively, and when the bank moves to foreclose on their house, she insists, in surprise, "I never signed any paper that said they could take my house like this" (102). On one hand, Carmine represents the vast majority of people who fail to understand the usurious complexity of banking systems and mortgages and, more loosely, the ambiguous nature of property ownership. On the other hand, she seems never even to try to understand how banking works, and she willfully abandons her family's finances to Charley, particularly the responsibility for making money. She reminds him that a "man brings money into the house. It's nice when a woman can help with that but it's a man's job" (39). Adherence to an essentialist view of gendered economics allows Carmine to disavow a shared responsibility for her family's problems and to insult her husband's masculinity when he can no longer support their consolatory, ambivalently peacemaking overconsumption.

Grimsley fashions the Strangers' dysfunctional domestic life to reflect that of the national marketplace. He uses the former to help to critique the latter, urging his readers to evaluate the Strangers' simplistic position so as to better understand the more diffusely complicated American business world. This is why Grimsley links Charley to a once major firm, having Charley work for Arthur Andersen as a financial consultant who persuaded hospitals to buy superfluous software. Charley achieved this not by trying to understand the most pressing problems facing hospitals as they tried to achieve their goals but by managing to "woo and court lots of hospital administrators and doctors, a painful process which included any number of gourmet meals at expensive restaurants" (36). Like Charley's relationship with his wife, these business practices created unhealthy partnerships that focused primarily on benefiting individuals who worked to feed their own avaricious appetites, an easier goal perhaps than "pulling together" to improve the communal healing functions of hospitals. To add insult to injury, these extravagances are not even fully enjoyed. They reflect painful practices presumably because the participants cannot respect each other or themselves, and so their luxuries are tainted with bad company, annoyance, and semiconscious guilt. Nonetheless, the business administrators benefit by not serving the larger needs and appropriate expectations of practicing doctors, nurses, and support staff, as well as those of the patients, for whom ideally the administrators should be working—we might think of the romanticized personal and professional relationship of Danny and Ford. Grimsley sets romance aside in *Forgiveness* to link the conniving accounting firm to hospital systems in order to foreground the often vital, as well as intensely emotional, costs at stake.

More generally, Grimsley suggests that the problems with Charley's and his associates' business practices are that they pervert their own markets: companies cannot recoup sufficient value from commodities for which they overpay, and individuals consume large salaries and massive benefits without giving enough in exchange. These accumulating exchanges create a greater unevenness, and this crooked market economy initiates a series of collapses that devastate the unprepared. Understanding this process, Charley realizes that his present problems are both a symptom of and a cause of the financial crisis: "the fall of Enron and Arthur Andersen acts as a kind of overture to the collapse of World-Com, to an economic slide that puts hundreds of thousands of people out of work. All this as a result of my having sold inferior software to too many hospitals nationwide. I therefore carry a general sense of being at fault for the whole mess" (41). This is a self-aggrandizing assessment, a sign of the hyperbolic nature of contemporary discourse, but Charley's public business and personal financial practices do symbolize larger national trends, which begin in urban financial capitals and spread like a stain across the nation. Like the SUV climbing the Manhattan skyscraper, these practices are unsustainable illusions that enable people to believe that they can attain materialistic heights that they cannot. Nonetheless, people indulge these fantasies. More troubling, if we follow Grimsley's connections among Charley's actions, national trends, and a commercial surrealism, is the likelihood that, rather than attempt to restructure the system, the nation will continue to treat markets in the same fashion, just as Charley continues to spend money after losing his job. The result, Grimsley posits, will be death and destruction, packaged and sold in ways that intrigue and distract to the point of impotence for national audiences.

Grimsley depicts, then, the dangerous siren attraction of the commercialized surrealism spouted by television media and films, which encourages individuals to indulge in a procrustean hermeneutic, in a method of interpretation that both consciously and unconsciously suspends reality, cutting people off from others and disguising how markets can cause pain. No matter how improbable, Charley can willfully convince himself that the actions and behaviors in modern media seem "completely real," like an SUV driving up a building (1). As Charley observes, "we think like the movies. What we don't see or don't believe or don't agree with falls out of the frame" (122–23). Although at times Charley metacritically considers this mode of thinking—and his use of "we" suggests that perhaps we all engage in the same self-delusion—he declines to revise it and thus reinforces his own constructed, selfish view of the world. In *Boulevard,* Grimsley used the eye-catching cinematic surrealism of pornography to illustrate how "think[ing] like the movies" could serve as a juvenile heuristic device (for Newell) and as a device that increased a violently fantastical solipsism (for Jack); in *Forgiveness,* Grimsley highlights the latter via television and movie culture. He indicates through Charley how without the ability to consider seriously and to empathize with others, we lose touch with other people's humanity, and this loss allows us to cause them psychological and even physical harm. Hence, when Charley's wife, Carmine, demands a divorce and amplifies her hypocritical verbal abuse of him, he brutally kills her and their son, unable to empathize with their perspectives or their ability to feel pain, which he has deliberately shoved out of focus in his frame of reference, just as he and his business partners shoved out the actual needs of hospitals and their patients and the jobs that people lose due to uneven commercial exchanges.

This mental myopia permits Charley to aggrandize his own perspective by drawing on the most inane elements of contemporary celebrity worship, such as a preference for scandal and fame over skill and reason. Charley imagines that his romantic troubles followed by his lurid murder of his wife will affiliate him with certain celebrities and propel him into the national spotlight. In a scene written from the perspective of Charley's pseudo-reality, its ostensibly realist style underlining Grimsley's satire of Charley's delusion, Charley believes that he has a tête-à-tête in a Starbucks with Nicole Kidman during which they offer each other compassion for their situations, a fantasy enabled by prominent tabloid reports of Kidman's own romantic problems in the early twenty-first century (14). Subsequently, Charley imagines participating in genial interviews with Katie Couric and Barbara Walters regarding his murder of his wife and envisions a "Lifetime Channel movie version" of his life where he is played by handsome stars, such as Dean Cain or Antonio Sabato, Jr. (10, 11). Charley knows little of these people, but the highly public commercialization of their lives underwrites the mental gymnastics that enable him to imagine realistically, that is, using selected factual details, their connection to him and for him to imagine that others might perceive him as similar to such men. Grimsley evolves here his critique of market exchanges: Charley has done little to deserve such public attention or the interest of any celebrities, but America's Hollywood-obsessed tabloid, television, and talk show culture, in which the public fawns over talented celebrities for trivialities and makes untalented people famous for barbarous behavior, nonetheless validates his expectations. Ironically, Charley is sophisticated enough to realize that Carmine must also have an individualized "movie version" of her life, but his obsessive self-interest cannot permit this realization to encompass Carmine's regrets and hopes in a fashion that will allow the couple to reconcile with any beneficially productive results.

While the violence of Charley's irresponsible, egotistical self-aggrandizement culminates in his murder of Carmine, its absurdity reaches its culmination when he considers what the reward for his behavior should be. In a fantasy scene structured as a television interview, Barbara Walters asks Charley what should happen to him, and Charley responds that he should be pardoned: "I should go free, and somebody should give me a really good job" (92). In context, Grimsley creates a remarkably funny moment as he characterizes both Charley's absurdly unfair expectations and his persistence in these expectations despite his realization that they are irrational, a realization evidenced by Charley when he senses, even in his fantasy, that the generally unflappable Walters would be stunned by this response (92). In a postmodernist fashion, Grimsley plays with the surreality of everyday realism—somewhat analogous to his treatment of realism in *Dream Boy*—for, while the majority of readers might be as stunned by Charley's audaciously unrealistic expectation as the fictional Walters, from Charley's perspective being rewarded with a new "good job" might actually seem like a credible prospect considering the golden parachutes and continued employment of so many involved in corporate scandals.

While the upper-middle-class suburban setting and heavily satirical, surrealistic form of *Forgiveness* might seem to set the novel apart from Grimsley's previous work, it is worth reading this novel in conjunction with *Mr. Universe* and *Boulevard* and even the earlier Tote-Crell novels and *Dream Boy*. Taken together, these narratives offer extensive meditations on motivations for violence and the need for socially responsible, moral pursuits of desire, even if Grimsley evokes the latter primarily through negative exempla. Self-absorption and an unwillingness to consider the needs and longings of others fuel the violence of Bobjay Crell; Nathan's father, Harland; and Roy's friend Burke, each of whom exhibits extreme failures of empathy and self-control that lead to sexual physical violence. Judy, Jack, Mark Duval, and Charley Stranger suffer from a similar selfishness, but the relative opportunities for freedom of expression and the potential to find more supportive communal networks offered by their urban and suburban settings heighten the needlessness of their violence because these opportunities could offer an escape from it, throwing into stark relief the social, emotional, intellectual, and psychological barriers erected by more rural poverty.

Even within urban settings, of course, Grimsley makes key distinctions. Significantly, he contains Judy's violence as she primarily harms only herself. By preventing her from fatally wounding others, Grimsley tries to prevent readers' disgust for her violent behavior from overwhelming any sympathy they might feel for how her particular gender and sexual nonconformities as well as her urban poverty lead to social rejections that exacerbate her self-destructive tendencies. In contrast, Jack, Mark, and Charley represent the greed and self-absorption of those whose wealth, education, and social status offer opportunities for movement and choices unavailable to those living in more impoverished circumstances, urban or rural.

More optimistically, the Muscle Man, Vick, Miss Sophia, and Newell represent the qualified, imperfect benefits of life in the city. The Muscle Man and Vick have the freedom to benefit from an urban quasi tolerance in order to build a new family structure. Even as Miss Sophia faces the indignities of queerphobia or transphobia, she courageously fashions an environment in which to refine her female identity. Newell, who encounters less prejudice, finds a wealth of occasions to expand his knowledge of the external world through books, buildings, and experiences that were not available, at least not as readily, in the small town where he used to live. This urban freedom allows Newell greater prospects for exploring new forms of consensual sensations, a process that indicates how intentions and informed consent can determine the morality of sexual behavior and help to distinguish between pleasure and pain. As Newell leaves New Orleans with the intention of traveling to other places, undoubtedly to other cities, in order to build on what he has learned, it is tempting to imagine that one day his path might cross with that of Roy and Nathan, at least, perhaps, in one iteration of their narrative.

CHAPTER 5

Fantasy and Science Fiction

Boulevard ends with travel as Newell, like so many of Grimsley's characters before him, prepares to pursue and to capitalize upon his expanding knowledge of the complexities of time, place, and the possible variations in sexualities, genders, and races in the human society around him. In a related yet distinct series of novels Grimsley plays with the generic conventions of fantasy and science fiction to expand the complexities of these possibilities and the social practices that they might create beyond the reality of our own world. Although, as Wendy Pearson has noted, "there have always been some [science fiction] stories which have touched on issues of sexuality in imaginative ways, often allegorically, these have until recently been vastly outweighed by the number of stories which take for granted the continued prevalence of heteronormative institutional practices—dates, marriage, the nuclear family and so on."[1] Refusing to take these practices for granted in his own fantasy and science fiction, Grimsley uses these distinct and yet related genres to explore, often in pragmatic ways, nonheternormative sexualities and practices and to reimagine more broadly how they connect to sequences of time, social customs, families, and spiritual beliefs, which, in turn, work to create a greater variety of what can actually count as normative standards in the first place.

In *Kirith Kirin* (2000), *The Ordinary* (2004), and *The Last Green Tree* (2006), Grimsley insists on the past, the present, and the future as mutually influential and as multiple as time and the sexual and social practices that take place within it become more capacious and multifaceted than Earth-bound humanity conventionally perceives them to be. While Grimsley examines similar concepts in *My Drowning* and *Dream Boy,* the freedoms of fantasy and sci-fi allow him to explore substantially larger expanses of chronology, space, and community than was possible in these earlier novels. Through depictions of fast-paced, sometimes instantaneous travel through millennia and between planets with diverse cultures, institutions, languages, and epistemologies, Grimsley assesses his characters' flawed individualism and their desire to forge communities amid the intertwining pressures of myth, history, received habits, new technologies, and religion. Here, as in Grimsley's interrelated narratives pertaining to the Tote-Crell family, characters must learn to forge new domestic spaces that inform their understanding of the choices they have made, could make, and will make to attain a qualified happiness despite the force of often hostile environments in which they are simultaneously insiders and outcasts. Finally, these fantasy and sci-fi novels, more than any others in Grimsley's expansive body of work, explore these themes to trace a long-term cultural shift from a blind faith in willfully ambiguous religious traditions to a more critical, scientifically based reliance on more secular human achievements and a secular morality open to critique.

Kirith Kirin

While Grimsley focuses on the uncertainty of memory in personal and family narratives in his Tote-Crell trilogy and the sexual repressions and liberations inherent in fallible biblical interpretations in *Dream Boy*, in *Kirith Kirin* he uses millennial time spans to interrogate more broadly the stability and the reliability of larger-scale foundational myths. He suggests the uncertainty of once certain origin narratives by presenting the world Aeryn as having unexpectedly deviated from its ostensibly divine natural order, thereby throwing into question the omnipotence of the goddess YY, supposedly the creator of Aeryn and its people. Whoever YY is, she initially distributed power over Aeryn to Kirith Kirin and to his sister Athryn Ardfalla in cycles, but this order has been disrupted by Athryn Ardfalla's centuries-long refusal to abdicate when her latest cycle came to an end. She allows the wizard Drudaen to circumvent the established order of their world in order to retain her power and in the process terrifies much of the populace into submission, implying the horrors that can result when humanity misguidedly and avariciously rejects a peaceful and natural, if never overly idealized, transition of power. Kirith Kirin finds help in his struggle to regain the throne from Jessex, a young boy raised to be a farmer until the Sisters of the Goddess reveal to him that he comes from a long lineage of wizards. The Sisters train Jessex in wizardry so that he can defeat Drudaen and reassert YY's divine mandate. As these narrative twists suggest, at the heart of this novel is Grimsley's urge to destabilize and to reinterpret received histories, an urge, expanded throughout his fantasy sci-fi series, to insist on the inherent obscurity of origin stories that define our understandings of the nation-state, of religious authority, and of our multifaceted and evolving ability to readjust to the world around us.

Grimsley pointedly begins *Kirith Kirin* on a note of retrospective doubt to emphasize the disputability of origin myths purporting to record the rise of larger-than-life authorities. Jessex's first sentence as narrator contradicts written accounts of his life prior to his religious and political ascendency among his people, the Jisraegan: "many lies are told about me now that I have become rich and famous . . . about my birth and childhood. . . . I can hardly credit even my own memories, but I know that most of what is written could not be true" (15). Jessex questions both verbal and textual accounts of his rise to power, affluence, and fame several millennia ago, while at the same time insisting that his own recollected versions must be taken as imprecise. At stake are imputations that both outsider and insider reports, including perhaps Jessex's own, intentionally mislead and that subsequent unintentionally misleading but nonetheless inaccurate reports attempt to chronicle the history in a fashion that authenticates and legitimates Jessex's rise to authority beginning when he is fourteen. As Jessex himself represents a bridge between the king and the Goddess's representatives, a bridge between the poles of Kirith Kirin and YY herself, his ambiguous origins throw an implicit, indirect doubt on the legitimating narratives that sustain Aeryn's secular and divine authorities. These characters overtly wield power as Jessex becomes a strong wizard, and many people follow Kirith Kirin as he fights to regain his kingdom and to reassert YY's supposedly divine order. Yet, through the novel's very first sentence, Grimsley works to subvert characterizations of the origins that license this power across generations.

This is not to suggest, however, that foundational myths or legends have no elements of truth in this world. Grimsley proposes rather that these narratives frequently contain details that must be separated and reevaluated for accuracy and reassessed in conjunction with relevant collated contexts. Through family discussions, for instance, Jessex learns of an uncle who vanished from Aeryn into the Arthen forest, "where many folks had vanished in bygone days, if stories were true" (16). These family memories clearly connect to larger community legends or to folktales, as Jessex's family puts his uncle's disappearance in the context of accounts of others' absence. Grimsley likewise links these family memories to the fireside and bedtime stories that Jessex's grandmother tells him regarding the "YY-Sisters," ancient "Wars of the Sorcerers," the original "Twelve who did not die" who established a Jisragen aristocracy, and the king who "had ridden into Arthen, to wait for the Queen to tire and call him out of the Woodland to rule again" (17). These tales are told in settings conventionally fit not just for folktales but for fairytales, complete with caveats that evoke an ancient unreliability—if the stories from "bygone days" are true—that transfers to the grandmother's vague late-night descriptions of primordial mysterious forests. Still, the grandmother's stories turn out to be partly accurate when Jessex's uncle suddenly arrives from the Arthen forest to claim Jessex to work in the shrine to YY at Kirith Kirin's camp. Grimsley thus prepares us to see how myths can transmit a historical perspective that provides, despite its incompleteness or inaccuracy, a basic understanding that Jessex will be able to use to orient himself when he finally meets the figures out of these stories. Like the "monkster" legend from *My Drowning* that reflects a local community's problems with alcoholism and violence or the biblical stories from *Dream Boy* that can legitimate homosexuality, the myths and legends in *Kirith Kirin* provide some insight into this world's long-evolving descent into political turmoil. Grimsley uses the conventions of the epic fantasy genre, moreover, to expand enormously both the geopolitical scope and the time frame that these allegorical truths can encompass beyond the local and beyond the relatively short existence of Christianity.

Grimsley uses these indeterminate legends to question our ability to determine the warrant of a divine authority itself. At the Arthen military camp where Jessex trains in religious traditions, he learns a ritual lamp ceremony that symbolically replicates how "YY-Mother sends darkness and light" even as "she is removed from both," a ceremony that he must repeat daily in public. The circumstances of this ritual reinforce the conception of YY as the establisher of a regular order of nature (for example, the cycles of morning and evening) and of a public life (for example, repeated communal gatherings), which do not necessarily bind her because she is "removed" from them. Consequently, this ritual helps to underwrite YY's authority by evoking her role as creator of the cosmos and a source of order, community, and stability. Yet even at this early stage of his career, Jessex realizes that this certifying narrative has a murky source, for the "lamp ritual is older than anybody remembers, going back at least as far as . . . when written Jisraegen history commenced" (66). As such, the authorizing potential of the ritual becomes questionable because of the uncertainty around the ritual's own origin. What, in other words, certifies the legend of the ritual that links it to YY and authorizes her authority? This uncertainty undermines the justification of YY's control over Jisraegan society, even as her practical religious and social influence remains intact and continues to signal Kirith Kirin's right to retake the throne from his sister.

One benefit to such uncertain origins, Grimsley suggests, is that they facilitate variabilities in regulatory traditions. "No one," Jessex observes, "should serve [YY's] shrine after attaining the nineteenth year, according to a custom as old as we are, though exceptions are made" (66–67). In rituals that gird other institutions and social structures, such as sexual, romantic, and familial relationships, standard conventions without a secure anchor likewise make room for exceptions and deviations in practice. Grimsley imagines variations in marriage practices, for instance, using the freedom of the fantasy genre to imagine the normalization of arrangements that take place only fairly covertly in our own world. In Aeryn, for instance, Jessex's parents "settled on the northern form of marriage, under which Papa agreed to share his house with [Jessex's mother], and to raise whatever children she bore under his roof, and each agreed to respect the other's right to occasional liaisons with others," and their "eldest child would inherit the farm after both of them were dead" (16). While this form of marriage replicates human traditions of heterosexuality, primogeniture, and patriarchy, it nonetheless breaks from a contemporary Western human heteronomativity by institutionalizing a sexual freedom from monogamy and normalizing a definition of parenthood not predicated on biology.

Grimsley uses this "northern" variation of marriage to prepare for his subsequent description of the legitimacy of same-sex marriages and their acceptability even among political and religious leaders, specifically Jessex and Kirith Kirin. Their ceremony, formally witnessed by others, includes a simple oath-taking and gift-giving: "I will live in you as you will live in me. I give you my promise with this gift" (300). Jessex and Kirith Kirin exchange presents linked to their families, inherited items, so their ceremony enacts not only their marriage but also their connections to each other's family. Their witnesses, moreover, make the ceremony a public contract. This works even in the face of some potential opposition, as after their marriage Kirith Kirin tells Jessex that there "are some folks, particularly southerners, who don't think men should lie down with men, or women with women" (311). By acknowledging the differences in regional mores, Grimsley keeps the Jisraegan society recognizably similar to that of present-day United States, where the South remains the region that most forcefully resists homosexuality. As such, he offers a trenchant critique of current sexual repressions in the United States, while simultaneously envisioning an alternative. For no one questions the legality of this version of the Jisraegan marriage ceremony, even as no one seems to sanction those few who disapprove of it. This scene therefore imagines in 2000 the institutionalization of gay marriage and, importantly, a version that works largely outside typical heteronormative and patriarchal concerns of lineage, as Jessex and Kirith Kirin never intend to produce children or to adopt. No one seriously suggests that this decoupling of marriage from reproduction will lessen the couple's desire to improve their world or that their marriage will destabilize a transition to a new state authority when either the king or his consort die. Finally, their marriage also validates the relationship of cross-generational men, as Jessex is just on the cusp of adulthood, almost sixteen at the time of their wedding, and Kirith Kirin has lived for thousands of years.

The fantasy genre, then, provides a unique means for Grimsley to evolve his interest in bringing mistreated, socially alienated men or adolescents into relationships with larger-than-life lovers. Jessex and Kirith Kirin, the latter a towering legend in Jisraegan history, represent a pair akin to Vick and the Muscle Man in *Mr. Universe,* Nathan and Roy in *Dream Boy,* or, in *Winter Birds,* Danny and the dreamlike River Man, who transforms into the problematic yet beautiful and affluent Ford in *Comfort and Joy* (305). The key difference is that Kirith Kirin is stronger and more powerful than these earlier lovers, and he can engage Jessex on more nearly equal terms and with far fewer sexual anxieties. Grimsley uses the flexible, world-creating possibilities facilitated by the fantasy genre to fashion a proximate equivalency of power between these lovers. The YY-Sisters train the one-time farm boy Jessex to be a potent wizard by creating a split timeline that allows him to train for expanses of untold time with "only a few hours" having passed in his world (106). As such, Jessex gains a status and a maturity as close to those of Kirith Kirin as is possible in their world, despite the latter's nominal rank and age. This fantasy world, although strategically constrained by its similarities to our world with regard to regional divisions, easily recognizable sexes and genders, and the centrality of romantic and companionate relationships, nonetheless provides Grimsley with the perfect genre to capitalize on Aristotelean probable impossibilities in order to bring together a physically and emotionally young but mentally mature adolescent and a physically perfect adult male lover, who has nonetheless had millennia of experience and is politically and socially powerful.

Because of this complicated time schematic, these lovers present a hyper-idealized reimagining of the adolescent and adult same-sex pairings inherited in Western culture by way of the Greeks while minimizing the need for moral objections that adhere to relationships with such a deceptively youthful partner. Reviewers were divided over the effectiveness of this strategy. Rejecting as irrelevant Grimsley's complex chronologies, David Tedhams lamented that this relationship is none the less pedophilic, and he criticizes what he considers an "implicit analogy" to the rapacious "Zeus/Ganymede myth," although he otherwise considers the novel "a great book."[2] Another anonymous reviewer, however, observed that in *Kirith Kirin* "Grimsley crafts an elegant tale of love, war, and magic in the epic fantasy tradition."[3] Most important, however, is how this couple's love joins romance to partnership so that the the two flourish as they live, work, and age together over hundreds of years, with less tension than lovers in Grimsley's other novels, their long-lasting, stable same-sex relationship succeeding in no small part because their society acknowledges it as a natural, consecrated, and valuable legal union.

The relationship between Kirith Kirin and Jessex also indicates how Grimsley's treatment of time has remained uniquely fluid and elastic in each novel. In *Dream Boy* and *My Drowning* he explored the tendency for time to expand or contract or divide as a result of how we contemplate or perceive it. In *Kirith Kirin* he uses the heuristic conception of magic to explain how a consciousness might create undefined stretches of experience within a single moment. When the Sisters train Jessex, for instance, his time with them "is a bubble" that they have made separate from normal time (106). Grimsley imagines here individuals' ability to manipulate, with significantly more individual agency and intention than in his earlier work, simultaneously parallel and analogous yet not quite equivalent unfoldings of time. Jessex discovers that "the trained mind can alter time's density, making a moment seem like a day, a week, a month." This ability enables this bubbling of time that creates intertwining but also somewhat independent parallels, allowing one to live years in a few hours and a few hours in years. As a corollary, Jessex gains the ability to explore in greater depth than most others the world around him and his own self. He reports, "I learned that the mind has deep rivers of memory and sensation whose existence one never suspects . . . that every moment of my life was stored in memory in perfect detail, that each memory could be recalled in its entirety" (170). This exact archive of life provides a unique type of eternity, as well of a near omniscience of and omnipotence over oneself. An outcome of this, in the novel, is that Jessex is able "to see with the mind alone . . . to release memory and, finally, to free portions of the spirit from the body for travel or work" on a variety of levels of consciousness (172–73). An ability to separate his mind, memory, or consciousness from his body allows Jessex to study ideas and actions in immense detail and to do so while performing other tasks, often without the interference of emotions or of a rationality constrained by a conventionally diachronic series of events. Essentially Jessex can perform complicated multitasking on microscopic levels across macroscopic time-space continuums.

While Grimsley relies on magic to describe these heightened levels of consciousness, his description resists totalizing supernatural explanations and is only partly spiritual as he roots it in sacred languages linked to a natural materiality. YY's Sisters train Jessex in a sacred language, and so his magic is associated with his understanding of divinity, a link emphasized by the second name the Sisters give Jessex, "Yron" or "God's claw" (156). Still, in *Kirith Kirin* magic requires the ability to manipulate special languages that immediately and intimately influence consciousness and the physical world. Consciousness and the physical world, Jessex learns, are so intimately intertwined that any separation of the two offers a false dichotomy that hampers a complete engagement with any environment. The most sacred language, which he learns from YY's Sisters, is called "Wyyvisar, a word that might be translated, 'waves weaving,'" a term evocative of the physical vibrations of sound waves, a music of molecules (122). Adepts learn to weave Wyyvisar words into song to create magic, since "magic is the act of making a harmony that alters the underlying music that is the basis for the world we know. . . . On the most basic level of magic, this act consists of naming an object with conviction," so singing multiple words with conviction adds complexity to the process (123). Magic in the novel, then, is an ability to create or reshape the way one considers the world and therefore the world itself through language and song, since these are the intrinsic basis of the material world, a molecular music. A more sophisticated ability to manipulate these languages and, through them, to develop new names, classifications, and narratives leads to ever greater power over oneself and over anything else, from the weather to the passage of time to people's perceptions and thoughts.

In many ways, Grimsley's description of this divinely authorized, musical magic resonates with classical and neoclassical philosophies that connect a heavenly "music of the spheres" to reverberations that should guide human actions. According to Pythogorean and Platonic traditions, the physical waves created by a celestial music or hymning reverberate in people's ears, activating their corporeal senses and guiding, however subtly, their behaviors.[4] Sound, including spoken language, and music thus form a thoughtful physical sway or predictable vibrations, a theory substantiated, in parts, by scientists such as Ernst Chladni, Wilhelm Weber, and others.[5] In a similar fashion, although with a more complexly creative power, Wyyvisar words have a direct physical connection to what they name. They blur the arbitrary boundaries between Saussure's conception of a sign, the signified, and a signifier and function analogously to J. L. Austin's performative speech acts, although with more immediate effects not just on consciousness and materiality but also on time.[6] When someone speaks Wyyvisar, a "wave is set in motion and that wave brings a change forward from the past to the present" (123). Grimsley's explanations of magic, with their reliance on the physical effects of sound, reminiscent of greatly amplified soundwaves, represent a fairly scientific way to insist on the real-world consequences of thoughts and speech, which never simply occur in a vacuum. Magic consequently functions not just as a mystical shortcut to action or even as an articulated hope that a higher power might deign to fulfill, as in some forms of prayer, but as a way of knowing and interacting with the world and with human minds in more complex intellectual, psychological, and physical ways.

As such, Grimsley insists on the necessity for training to refine any innate talent to manipulate the physical effects of magic. Jessex begins the novel with a close connection between his mind and animals. In his youth, he is an unusually good shepherd, with animals knowing what he wants "without [his] having to tell them," and his ability to communicate with a horse allows him to pass easily a riding test that an oracle has instructed his uncle to set for him (22, 28). Jessex's magical ability to commune with animals and to satisfy the requirement of the oracle, despite his seemingly lowly background, place him in the larger literary tradition of young heroes who face initiation tests to prove their maturity and worth and that often signal the hero's actually quite exalted lineage: indeed, after investing immense time in teaching and training Jessex, the Sisters reveal that he is the descendant of a renowned sorceress who had to give up her child anonymously in order to protect it.[7] This narrative structure demonstrates heroes learning from experience and, in Grimsley's version, emphasizes how education and practice must bolster natural talent and lineage—the importance of education being a theme that resonates throughout Grimsley's writing, again connecting his fantasy world to the realism or surrealism of his other novels. Thus, Jessex's natural ability to turn thought into material action comes to more mature fruition after his extensive work with YY's Sisters.

While Grimsley tempers *Kirith Kirin*'s fantasy elements by emphasizing the learnable, almost scientifically explainable causes and effects of magic, following the conclusion to the main narrative he takes an emphatic turn toward science fiction by adding appendices compiled by a fictional scholar that offer a metacritical reflection on the main body of the novel. In the story world of the appendices, *Kirith Kirin* gets revealed as Jessex's memoir, which has been translated from Jisraegen and commented on by Jedda Martele, who lives some "nine hundred years" after the events detailed in the memoir and who comes from a different people, the "Hormling" (553). Jedda refers to unnamed works by scholars, to science, and to "Hormling scientists," and she makes clear that she comes from a society that relies upon technology as opposed to magic (532, 542). This cultural difference implicitly shapes her compilation of the six appendices that attempt to approach a foreign society empirically by providing a glossary, an outlined summary of Jisraegen history, a critique of the Jisraegen calendar, a description of key magical places, a discussion of a "theory of magic as currently codified by the Hormling," and a translator's note (547). Grimsley's late introduction of Jedda recontextualizes his own fantasy novel and Jessex's memoir by refocusing it, albeit briefly, through another, rather less fantastically fashioned analytical lens.

In part, Jedda's analytical apparatus provides Grimsley's readers with useful references to a substantial text. More important, it reinforces at the book's end Grimsley's double-edged insistence on questioning the accuracy of received foundational narratives and on considering these narratives to be indispensable social and historical guides if approached critically. Jedda laments that within "*Kirith Kirin* there are contradictory historical assertions" and that "no archaeological studies" have been tolerated in contemporary Jisraegen territory (532). She acknowledges, however, despite her cultural preference for contradiction-resolving empirical evidence, that no one in Jisraegen territory "doubts that this tale is anything but history," regardless of its inconsistencies, and she admits that her own people have "come closer to grasping the reality that this may be a true history, and that magic may be real" (554). Jedda and the Hormling, it seems, have come to rely on alleged myths to understand the foreign Jisraegen culture, hence her undertaking to translate Jessex's narrative. History and myth then, Grimsley suggests, can be two approaches to a series of events that reveal more information when approached through multiple lenses, each of which focuses on different details. Jedda's preference for an objective historicism, for instance, allows her cautiously to understand magic as something that "may be real," while Jessex considers it primarily as substantiation of the importance of YY and her religion. Still, when we compare Jessex's studious descriptions of magic and Jedda's attempts at a scientifically engaged classification of this subject, we see that magic and science become two means of engaging the world separated more by rhetoric than by fact or practice, a theme that Grimsley develops in greater detail through Jedda in *The Ordinary.*

The Ordinary

Grimsley picks up Jedda's story in *The Ordinary* to explore the tense intercultural encounters between the Hormling and the Erejhen (an evolved spelling and pronunciation of Jisraegen) growing out of their divergent pursuits in, respectively, advanced computer systems with industrial production methods and a deceptively primitive religious magic with a more artisanal economy. In *The Ordinary,* as Devon Thomas has noted, Grimsley combines science fiction and fantasy to critique "humanity's tendency to discount what it can't measure" and to explore "the clash between cultures and how communication—specifically language—can change perceptions and even reality."[8] Indeed, Grimsley is particularly concerned with examining perceptions of reality that change due to encounters with unexpected definitions and classifications. He takes great interest in imagining scientific terms and advances and in imagining what Paula Luedtke has called "a beautifully developed spirituality," both of which the novel uses to consider why and how societies such as the Hormling and the Erejhen choose to engage each other, each jockeying for dominance over the other.[9]

Indeed, the underlying purpose of this jockeying is tied to Grimsley's exploration of the relationships among science, spirituality, nationalism, and origins. Steve Berman has praised Grimsley for involving his "characters in the search for higher meaning," lamenting that "too often speculative fiction writers steer clear of philosophy and theology for fear of alienating readers," a fear that Grimsley confronts head on to examine how religious practices can permeate national, social, and economic contexts.[10] As he does so, *The Ordinary* becomes a more pointed critique of twenty-first-century U.S. society in particular as he presents the humanlike Hormling as an imperial power with a deeply flawed social, political, and economic hierarchy built on the twin principles of warfare and welfare. The wealthy classes of Hormling use both these principles to sustain their existence by distracting the general populace from the possibility of revolt. Affluent Hormling create distractions by perverting technological advances for the purposes of violence and social repression and through the destruction of the natural environment of a planet to which they very likely had fled after having inflicted similar traumas on a previous world. Grimsley carries this uncertainty of origin through to his simultaneous depictions of the racial diversity of the Jisraegen and to his investigation into the unreliable foundation myths of nations and of spiritual beliefs, which themselves are so frequently intertwined.

The Ordinary begins by critiquing how the Hormling have grown naively accustomed to perpetual hostilities. Grimsley reintroduces Jedda Martele on Senal, the Hormling home world, as she watches "a flatscreen filled with pictures from the distant war" while waiting to travel to Irion, Aeryn's evolved name, on an exploratory mission for her government (13). Jedda's unsettling comfort with this war quickly becomes apparent as she notes that this "footage had a wonderful freshness to it, though it was at least fifteen years old, the distance from Tret to Home Star. Here was proof the war was still alive" (13–14). Jedda is not disturbed by the images; instead, her sense of the freshness of the decade-and-a-half-old footage, added to her characterization of the fighting as alive, signals her familiarity with and acceptance of a continuous state of hostilities as she immediately imagines that old battles have given way to new ones rather than to peace. Considered from a literally flattening, filtering screen and from an enormous distance, the distorted, outdated facts, exhibited as current and yet without the immediacy of a battlefield, enable the news media to ensure that a relatively painless understanding of the feud remains almost omnipresent in her homeland, which results in a form of complacency. So long a part of the Hormling's background environment, this conflict, although constituted of death and destruction, has assumed a largely unquestioned and self-perpetuating life of its own.

The Hormling's comfort with this self-perpetuation is particularly ironic as the war presents a dead-end road to self-destruction through an uncritical use of mass-produced technology. Significantly, the Hormling are battling their own machines, which have "rebelled against" them, and they find that they "can't win" against their own technology (72, 118). This rebellion proves especially problematic as every Hormling carries a mandatory "stat" device, partly implanted in them, that will "input, upload, and download" individuals' experiences to a hive of collective information and that can simultaneously help individuals to regulate emotions and moods (31, 67). If people receive bad information, they can always adjust "the level of sedative chemicals in their bodies" via their stats, a system reminiscent of Aldous Huxley's dystopian soma rations in *Brave New World,* only more insidious because it is linked directly to the Hormling information system (17). For a society so reliant on electronics and machines, this "Metal War" represents an internecine struggle against the Hormling's way of life (72). Fighting against this sort of technology, while continuing to rely so heavily on it, symbolizes the pursuit of a self-destructive impasse, like a snake eating its own tail.

This war nonetheless serves the Hormling ruling class by distracting its subjects from the social and environmental inequities on Senal itself. Grimsley argues against industrial environmental destruction most thoroughly in *The Last Green Tree,* but he anticipates those arguments in *The Ordinary* by using Senal to critique a divisive economy that profits a ruling class as it degrades a tightly controlled underclass and wreaks ecological havoc. The Orminy, the Hormling "ruling caste," have shaped their society so that, despite its production of portable computer systems, so affordable that almost everyone has one, overcrowding dominates, with the result that even many relatively well-off individuals have to live for months in underground apartments, while the massive population living in poverty subsists in communal public housing (14, 13). This public housing is part of what the Hormling call "the minimum," an entitlement "to food and shelter under certain conditions" combined with the ability to earn extra "money for the luxuries," like "a home of one's own" outside the "communal subclave[s]," a term for the underground group living space derived perhaps from the words "sub" and "enclave" or from the Latin "sub" and "clave," indicating someone under the key or, more colloquially, imprisoned (149, 80). This subsistence welfare provides a justification for the Hormling version of mass industrialism, which enables it, and pacifies those who refuse or who cannot obtain jobs offered by Orminy-controlled government "ministries" or "Factions" or even by small businesses (149). These jobs themselves serve as a deceptive safety valve as the Orminy's control over information, the political system, and travel consistently stifle the increased income, influence, and individual agency that such jobs promise. Even Jedda, who has grown relatively wealthy by trading Erejhen goods, still frequently lives underground. Equally as troubling is how the mass industrial production supported by this population comes at the cost of natural resources. These resources all have to be divided among "thirty billion or so" people, with only the Orminy able to afford a significant share of wood, water, and access to open air (245). Thus, the distant war provides a welcome distraction from contemplating these systematic inequities at home.

Grimsley suggests, however, that such distractions often provide only temporary solutions the inefficacy of which leads to more violent and self-destructive tactics. The Hormling war and Senal's increasing lack of natural resources eventually cause the Orminy to engage Irion, which has plenty of space and natural resources. Grimsley structures this engagement to demonstrate how economic and intellectual exchanges can cover an arrogantly self-defeating militaristic imperialism. As Jedda surveys the distant war on the "flatscreen," she waits to accompany a mission from Senal to Irion (now ruled by Jessex via his plenipotentiary, a woman named Malin) through the Twil Gate, which appeared as a link between the two worlds about "twenty years" prior to the novel's beginning (13, 14). In this time trade has developed so that the Hormling benefit from the natural materials and artisanal production of Irionian goods such as cloth and textiles, while Irion populations, both the Anin and the dominant Erejhen peoples, gain access to Hormling machines (27). The Orminy bring Jedda on this mission because she has learned to speak Erejhen and Anin (36). Initially the Orminy claim that the mission is simply "to explore" and to lobby for "increased trade," but Jedda quickly realizes that the mission is to prepare "to invade. To colonize" Irion, to take its land, its wood, and its water by force (37, 63). When the Hormling delegation loses contact with Senal, the Orminy send a warship on a search party, breaking their pledge not to send more people and causing Irion representatives to disable the ship and to capture its crew peacefully with surprising ease. An Orminy representative notes that "this could be considered an act of war," meaning "the detaining of the three Hormling, of course, and not the entry of a military aircraft into this peaceful country," the rights of which the Orminy disregard (54). Having made false claims to Malin and even to their own emissaries to gain access to Irion, the Orminy purposefully misinterpret a defensive action as aggressive and send numerous seacraft, airships, and warplanes, all of which Malin destroys except for one plane, which she returns to Senal as a warning (84). Grimsley unfolds these events to indicate how even individuals such as Jedda, interested in relatively mutually profitable economic and intellectual exchanges, can be easily and unwittingly coopted for avaricious, uncritical, and even aggressively self-defeating purposes.

Grimsley also suggests here how an arrogant overreliance on one conception of technology can blind a society to still more effective forms of power. Overconfident in their warships, hovercrafts, and stats, the Orminy naively regard Irion expertise as primitive. Capable of recognizing only advances in electronics or engineering, the Hormling have difficulty accepting that the Erejhen could have blocked their stat communications on Irion, and the Hormling delegation's military official insists that the first disabled warplane must have simply malfunctioned (32, 55). Disregarding this warning, the Orminy send in an entire fleet and lose it. They also lose control of their homeland, for, as Jessex eventually reveals to Jedda, he himself created the magical Twil Gate, which the Orminy had hoped to use to invade Irion, so that the Erejhen could themselves invade Senal, to "carry what we can do . . . into your world" (205). The Orminy's refusal to acknowledge a powerful agency behind magical events because of a myopic rhetoric of development based on classifications derived primarily from industrialism and mechanical and computer engineering results in their unexpected erosion of influence.

The Hormling's arrogant discounting of the Erejhen's descriptions and understanding of their own culture provides a pointed development of Grimsley's interest from *Kirith Kirin* in evaluating signposts of truth in generally questionable origin myths. In present-day Irion, Jessex has withdrawn from everyday governance, which he leaves to his chief pupil, Malin, in order to study magic more extensively. Consequently the Hormling hear of Jessex, but because they have not seen him they mistake his immense power for a fabrication, to their own detriment. As one of Jedda's Hormling friends had suggested regarding early Erejhen warnings against invasion and their references to Jessex's power: "The message is too simple for us . . . we can't understand it, because we've decided they're primitive and that [Jessex] is probably mythical. But all these people believe he's real. They talk about him like they saw him yesterday" (57). Only when Malin, using the skills she has learned from Jessex, unequivocally demonstrates magical power by destroying triumphs of Hormling manufacturing and weaponry does she prove that the Erejhen's seemingly unreal expertise can dominate Hormling machines and that there were truths in the myths.

Grimsley's portrayal of machines and engineering, it is worth noting, does not stem from an antiscientific or from a retrogressively proagrarian ideology. He consistently advocates for the importance of education and favorably portrays medical doctors and hospitals in his Tote-Crell novels. Yet, he also consistently advocates for the differently introspective, analytical importance of the humanities, which offer their own valuable rhetorical and technical ways of knowing. In *Comfort and Joy,* for instance, Ford saves lives and gains wealth through the scientific practice of medicine, yet Danny, who acts and sings and reads outside professional contexts, is more emotionally and psychologically comfortable. Things work best when these ways of knowing are intertwined, as is the case when Ford and Danny happily work and live together or when Ellen Burley takes great satisfaction from the Saturn car she owns in *My Drowning,* an example of machines and science facilitating emotional and psychological independence (203).

Using science and magic in *The Ordinary,* Grimsley works to theorize how different ways of knowing might be first shaped and subsequently reshaped by evolving environments. As Jessex eventually tells Jedda regarding the Hormling, "you developed your science to explain, in part, the movements of heavenly bodies, which you observed to be regular, though complex. The order you saw in the heavens led you to search for order elsewhere. . . . I think we were shaped to develop the talents that we have developed" (202). Just as the rhythmic movements of Senal's sky inspired select Hormling to develop mathematically based epistemologies to discern an order in their environment that they could manipulate, so Irion/Aeryn's differently natured world inspired select Erejhen/Jisraegen to develop a harmonic or sound-based epistemology, which they call magic, that taught them to use unique singing languages to shape the forces around them. Jessex elaborates when he hypothesizes for Jedda that YY made his world "to shape a consciousness that could use a certain kind of language, a certain kind of thought. The consciousness is already the frame of reference by which you and I each move forward through time, there is already a certain level of binding of time into matter in the natural order. What I do is a step beyond that, a binding of events into the present moment, events that I will to happen" (203). Extrapolating from Jessex's theories, divinely bestowed or innate skills that are linked to consciousness and environment can evolve as changes over time can affect the matter of any given space, which can in turn reshape the potential to search for new sorts of order and to develop new ways of knowing.

Vital to this theory, as Jessex suggests, is that language and rhetoric create categories of definitions or classifications, such as science or magic or religion, that enhance the power to form narratives that allow us to review and to reshape our reality. Jessex, for instance, changes the seemingly random sky of Irion to work like a clock, like the sky of Senal, as part of building the Twil Gate, which links the two worlds and which will eventually bring the magic of Irion into Senal (199, 200). This process of cultural and environmental intermixing will inevitably reveal additional forms of knowledge through an expansion of language and thought, as Malin indicates when she notes that people of Irion begin to think differently after Jessex regulates the movements of the sky (346). Consequently, a simplified but not inaccurate description of the way

Grimsley conceives of Jessex's power is to say that it derives from an ability to manipulate the natural environment and to create increasingly complex, verifiable, and convincing stories that cause his people to reevaluate or to find new orders in the word around them.

Intrinsic to Jessex's theory is not just rhetoric and an engagement with reality but also an investigation into faith, spirituality, and the nature of what gets conceived of as divine. While in *Kirith Kirin* Jessex questioned origin myths, in *The Ordinary* the encounters between Senal and Irion cause him to question the very nature of YY and her place in the universe. As he tells Jedda, he has begun to think that "the universe" is "far more ancient" than YY, who might simply be a superior being "in possession of a science so far beyond" even the Hormling's "that it seems like magic" to both peoples (203). YY may have created worlds but she is most likely not an omnipotent or omniscient, much less a solitary, original creator. Jessex supposes that she is closer to the Hormling or Erejhen, "maybe she's simply something far older and far more knowledgeable than we are . . . like these Hormling might become, if their technology and science go on improving to their limits. Maybe that's what a god is to begin with," namely a far more knowledgeable but not necessarily infallible or fundamentally moral being (348). YY almost certainly created the original "forty thousand" Jisraegen, an origin story detailing the beginning of Jisraegen society, but after visiting Senal Jessex realizes that the Hormling could very likely "assemble the random DNA of forty thousand people, cause them to be born and to mature," a form of biological cloning (201). Moreover, Grimsley raises the implication that YY merely extended work already existent in the universe, as the Anin and Hormling are "genetically kin" and consequently the Erejhen and the Hormling are also likely related, a relationship implied in part by their related religions (78). YY seems to need, then, the Jisraegen/Erejhen for some reason, which Grimsley specifies in *The Last Green Tree*. The point in *The Ordinary* is that while YY can manipulate advanced technologies, she is somewhat limited and therefore had Jessex trained so that he could bridge Senal and Irion. As such, YY seems to be not just more imperfect or constrained than first imagined in *Kirith Kirin* but also somewhat aggressive, as she wants Jessex and indirectly Malin to invade Senal.

Considering these themes, in addition to being speculative spiritual fiction, *The Ordinary* becomes a science fiction mystery. What is the relationship between all these races and between Senal and Irion, bridged by the Twil Gate? Are there genetically related races scattered throughout the universe that might foreshadow potential physical or social evolutions for each other? What might one race learn from studying its distant relations? Why would a deity that had supposedly scattered these peoples and places want them to reconnect? From a narrative perspective, these mysteries prepare for *The Last Green Tree;* from a speculative perspective, the mystery takes on a primary poignancy because Grimsley gradually clarifies that the Hormling themselves are descended from humans. The Hormling's own origin story is that they arrived on Senal via a ship called "*Merced,*" which they mercifully took from Earth after the latter had become uninhabitable. Some Hormling suggest that this "story's from so long ago" that "there's no way to arrive at any truth that's in it" (139). Grimsley's own cautiously critical approach to setting up and then substantiating the partial truths of Jisraegen legends in *Kirith Kirin* suggests that there is truth in the Hormling myth. Consequently, Grimsley employs the Hormling to imagine what might happen to humans should they have to abandon Earth, perhaps due to industrial and ecological disasters analogous to those that the Hormling inflict on Senal. The Hormling society, with its retrenched socioeconomic castes, its misuse of technology, and its ecological disasters, warns against repetitively self-defeating human tendencies, somewhat akin to Grimsley's critique of avaricious economic structures promoted by the twenty-first-century U.S. media in *Forgiveness*.

Building on these speculations and mysteries, Grimsley uses the pervasive religious and socioeconomic structures of both Senal and Irion to suggest the problematically subtle and unavoidable influence of little-understood divinities on identity, bureaucracies, and politics. On Senal, the primary Hormling religion revolves around the deity Krys. Some Hormling take the faith very seriously; among these are the cult followers of a prophet who "preached that Krys" had brought the Hormling to Senal "to find a hidden paradise," an intimation of the beautiful if hardly paradisal world of Irion (78). Others treat the faith more loosely. Jedda, for instance, is familiar with key religious texts and is one of the "krys-believers," even if for her "the way of krys was more of her upbringing and not a tradition that she practiced" (77, 79). She is aware nonetheless that certain hours of the day have "religious implications," and she occasionally offers up a prayer (79). This latter information comes from the narration rather than from Jedda's speech or direct thoughts, and it consequently indicates how, although religion may not be at the forefront of her mind, it provides the background context for a significant portion of her thinking, as it does for many of her fellow Hormling. Indeed, Grimsley describes how each Hormling has a first name and a "krys name," a formula analogous to so-called Christian names on Earth. On Senal, a "krys name" indicates one's social or political position; a name with at least ten letters indicates a "high ranking" position or one superior to the positions of those with shorter names (20, 56). This ranking system both evidences and sustains how religion underwrites aspects of daily Hormling life in ways so familiar that they pass by almost unnoticed and therefore unchallenged, from perceptions regarding the time of day to an individual's social and political status. On Irion, religion permeates daily life still more overtly. Jessex Irion (his second name "Yron" evolves to "Irion" over time) is both a religious and a political leader, and Jedda notes that even everyday "government officials in the Erejhen bureaucracy underwent a religious training," such that a cleric might deal with a dispute between "trading partners" (79). The religion centered on YY thus permeates everything from Irionians' worship to their commercial practices to Irion's national identity.

Since Grimsley tackled the variously liberating and oppressive traditions of received Christianity in earlier novels, such as *Comfort and Joy* and *Dream Boy,* we might consider these as an interpretive guide for analyzing religion in *The Ordinary.* These contexts signal the benefits and the troubling pervasiveness of religion both on Senal and on Irion. Religion in *The Ordinary* seems void of misogyny and homophobia, which provides a relatively refreshing and liberating perspective of the only partially achieved potential for humanity's own spiritual institutions. Religious pervasiveness, however, becomes problematic when the moral omniscience of the guarantor of the religion, namely the deity, is uncertain. A major underlying principle of all societies' governmental, religious, and socioeconomic structures ought, Grimsley implies, to be reexamined after those societies acknowledge the problem of an organized faith structured around inherited interpretations of insufficiently contextualized beliefs, such as the Krys cult's theory of a "hidden paradise" and beliefs in the divinity of YY.

Grimsley uses these religious characteristics to critique the twenty-first-century influences of Christianity, specifically. The Hormling, the Anin, and the Erejhen all undoubtedly draw on Christian social practices, a characterization that suggests a cultural if not necessarily a genetic relationship between these races and humanity. Grimsley's imagined religions, for instance, all value spiritual words that relate to YY, which is pronounced, we learn from Jedda's appendix to *Kirith Kirin,* "Ee" (531). YY is almost certainly etymologically related to "Christ" via its forerunner "Krystos" from the Greek "Χρίστός," pronounced "Kree-stos." Reinforcing this onomastic correlation is Grimsley's interest in etymological changes and mergers over time—"Yron" from *Kirith Kirin,* for instance, which means "God's claw," has become "Irion" in *The Ordinary,* and this evolution signifies both Jessex's second name and the land that used to be called "Aeryn," which presents a possible cognate to "Irion" and reinforces the theocratic rule of this land. This lays the groundwork for perceiving Christian influences, however indirect and distant, on the Hormling "krys-believers" and the Erejhen "Krii," a "high-ranking" order of a priestly "Prin" class created by Jessex, as discussed in *The Ordinary* (41). Grimsley shapes these influences to imply that the same doubts regarding moral authority that Jessex Irion raises regarding the nature of YY and her institutions might apply to Christianity and its institutions as well. Consequently, Grimsley encourages us to recognize the morally problematic and perhaps unjustifiable pervasiveness of Christian influences in our own governmental bureaucracies, commercial institutions, and cultural practices, no matter how subtly they may operate.

Still, all of Grimsley's skepticism is not necessarily reproving. Some of it is more ambivalently admiring and exploratory, imagining how humanity's gendered and racial social structures might evolve over thousands of years. As in *Kirith Kirin,* women in *The Ordinary* are warriors and political leaders to the same degree as men, as evidenced by the invasive yet capable female pilot who flew the captured Hormling plane into Irion and by both the arrogant Tarma and the more thoughtful Malin, political leaders of the Hormling and the Erejhen, respectively (55). As these characters' roles indicate, neither on Senal nor on Irion do authoritative public positions seem to be gendered or sexed as hangovers from outdated traditions.

Grimsley also imagines unique mixtures of races in the Jisraegen and particularly in the Hormling, humanity's most direct descendants, to recall how social division can persist beyond gender and skin pigment. On Irion, people "ranged from ivory to ebony," but social divisions are generally structured according to ways of practicing magic or by regionalisms rather than by skin color (41). The Hormling, meanwhile, represent "the blend of many races of people who had come to Senal a long time ago," and "most people" have "the same color," a "creamy brown," with "similar features, including a slight almond cast to the eyes" (44). Jedda herself has "brown skin and eyes," and, to anticipate a bit, when YY appears to Jessex, she will be "silky brown" (*TO* 242–43; *TLGT* 348). Throughout *The Ordinary,* Grimsley never notes the existence of one dominant human racial heritage, although brown skin suggests the substantial presence of African, Arab, Indian, Pakistani, and/or Spanish heritages among the Hormling, and he never attempts to eradicate cultural pluralism, which in this world stems from regionalisms, diverse faith practices, and socioeconomic divisions, without skin color as a central focus. He presents this not as a cause for emphatic lament or for celebration but as the result of circumstances that facilitated progress in interracial relationships to the point where skin colors and diverse physical features combined in new ways. His nonchalant characterization of this evolution, alluded to almost in passing, brings to the fore and conventionalizes the mixed-race identities of an already enormous segment of Earth's population.

As an extension of these racial amalgamations, cross-generational homosexuality and even pansexuality continue to be normal, calmly accepted practices in *The Ordinary.* This is particularly true on Irion, where Jedda and Malin become lovers despite their differences in home worlds and age. This replicates for two women the hyperidealized combination of youth and maturity inherent in the relationship between Jessex and Kirith Kirin, just as it provides a balance to the diversely exploitative relationship between the older Louise and the pubescent Millie from *Boulevard*. When Jedda and Malin first meet, Jedda is "nearing seventy," past her "first youth and into the second, as they say" on Senal, where Hormling generally average two-century life spans, while the Erejhen Malin has already lived about "a thousand years" (80, 197, 350). These women present the primary love story that helps to propel the narrative of *The Ordinary,* which serves to centralize and normalize their relationship. Jedda, moreover, begins her relationship with Malin after engaging in affairs with a number of men, an acknowledgment of Jedda's ability to have liked, even if only for a moment, the physicality of at least one man before finding a woman to whom she was more powerfully attracted (56). While Grimsley has also then normalized this limited pansexuality and has used the expanded lifetimes of Jedda and Malin to reconceive the benefits of cross-generational, even cross-racial relationships, he curiously chose not to continue his exploration of trans identities as a valuable part of a social population, as he had so usefully done in *Boulevard,* although we might perhaps see this in his future science fiction.

Like so many science fiction authors, then, although with his own particular emphases, Grimsley uses *The Ordinary* to speculate on the future of humanity in order to imagine how its present social norms might transform over time. One Hormling, while discussing the similarities that emphasize the differences between Senal and Irion, remarks on the irony that "what's ordinary in one world is so extraordinary in the other" (136). In practice, Grimsley shapes both Senal and Irion to highlight the irony that concepts such as ecological sensitivities, critical religious queries, gender equality, and an acceptance of diverse sexual practices across races, sexes, and genders are still perceived by so much of twenty-first-century humanity as extraordinary enough as to seem almost alien when they could be, and in many instances are actually becoming, so wonderfully ordinary, so normal. In Grimsley's fantasy and science fiction, the very ordinariness of diverse sexualities, the presence of women in powerful positions, and racial mixing, to cite only three examples, should make us reflect on the extraordinary circumstance that these practices still cause so much violence and strife in our world today, albeit less than previously.

In this vein, the final moments of *The Ordinary* offer a hope for continued change through a faith, however shaken, in religious evolution and in a deity perceived as benevolent, however little understood she might be. In a moment of turmoil toward the novel's end, Jedda sees an "old woman" who imparts to her a "feeling of well-being, of perfection," and of gentleness, and whom Malin later identifies as YY (360). Jedda consequently joins Malin and Irion in their desire to have the Erejhen invade Senal in order to bring YY and her institutions to the Hormling. Their hope, variously understood by each of these characters, is that by finally bridging Senal and Irion they might fashion a "new world" with a gentler, more perfect future for each of its peoples (366). The result of this brave "new world" is what Grimsley explores in *The Last Green Tree.*

The Last Green Tree

Brave new worlds, unfortunately, seldom turn into the utopian paradises for which reformers work but often run into problems due to reformers' imperfect efforts to improve present systems and to the resultant reactionary backlash. In *The Last Green Tree,* Grimsley indirectly reflects these themes from Aldous Huxley's dystopian *Brave New World* and from William Shakespeare's *The Tempest,* from which Huxley took his title, to examine how Jedda and Malin's attempts to improve Senal and Irion backfire as substantial socioeconomic restructurings ironically promote a still farther-flung ecologically destructive imperialism and even slavery. In addition to these conflicts, Grimsley draws on his characterizations of knowledge and power from *Kirith Kirin* and *The Ordinary* to construct what Regina Schroeder has called "a fascinating, grand-scale dichotomy of magic and science."[11] Continuing to explore the differences and similarities between these two epistemologies of power, Grimsley intensifies the stakes by imagining what one reviewer rightly called a "large-scale politics seasoned with gore and desperation" by depicting a degree of carnage and spiritual anxiety not as evident in the previous novels.[12] For to complicate heightened socioeconomic crises, in *The Last Green Tree* the previously unknown god Rao appears to challenge the moral authority and the governing influence of YY herself, whom Rao exposes as one of several ruthless beings that cruelly exploit human lives and planets in their own struggles for power. In the end, then, Grimsley suggests that any moral authority, however imperfect, must rest with the Erejhen, Anin, and Hormling and, thus, implicitly, with the human desire to search for knowledge that can inspire self-determined acts of decency irrespective of divine approval or appreciation.

One of the overriding goals of *The Last Green Tree,* set three centuries after *The Ordinary,* is to explore the difficulties in alleviating entrenched socioeconomic disparities in antagonistically hierarchical societies. Since conquering Senal, Malin, supported by her consort Jedda, has reduced the inherited social power and wealth once consistently abused by the Orminy, who lost most of their political power following the Erejhen invasion. Despite these reforms, the Orminy retain certain privileges that they continue to abuse. At his recent birthday party, Fineas "Figg" Bemona-Kakenet, "the eldest male of the eldest

Orminy house," murdered a former friend and justified the action as "perfectly legal" because his "family was licensed for a certain number of assassinations per year," a position he bolstered with the ostensibly moral maxim that "old laws are always the best" (97, 98). Figg's highly publicized legalized decadence, a use of a right for private purposes that do not benefit the state, helps to "set off the Common Fund Reforms," which Malin creates to dismantle still more of the Orminy's remaining privileges (97).

Disagreeing that longevity correlates to practicality or to moral justice, Malin claims much of the Orminy's wealth for the state and prohibits substantial inheritances. As Figg complains, she begins "taking everybody's money. Over a certain amount. And she's taking property," and people have to "give [money] up" when they die (16). The Common Fund Reforms reappropriate money primarily for relieving Senal's "Reeks"—what in *The Ordinary* were called "crèche[s]"—places where "people lived in public spaces, jammed body to body with hardly a moment of privacy, let alone comfort or safety," which had previously "enabled the rest of the world to live in a state of relative spaciousness and provided fodder for any number of other appetites of the upper class" (107). Malin's reforms achieve some success, in ways that the Orminy minimum never did, because the Common Fund eschews subsistence-level welfare and enables ambitious individuals to escape the Reeks, presumably named for their horrid smell, by opening shops and by "investing in a place in a colony" away from Senal (243). Nonetheless, Orminy such as Figg continue "to live very well" on the money that they have left, especially Orminy who immigrate to areas not yet affected by Malin's initiatives, Grimsley's critique of regressive welfare systems and tax havens (16, 18). Consequently, Malin uses her reforms to support upward mobility rather than stasis, even as she limits the scope of her reforms so as to ease each change and to avoid pushing the Orminy to revolt rather than to just complain.

Malin's limited reforms become increasingly problematic, however, as they result in an interplanetary imperialism that causes ecological destruction and a violent uprising in one of Senal's colonies. Malin relieves Senal's overpopulation and underemployment by using the new Common Fund to facilitate the colonization of Aramen, one of the Orminy's favored foreign tax havens. When Figg, for instance, abandons Senal for Aramen, where he can still "will his property to Keely," a boy adopted from the Reeks and his only immediate family, Figg's entourage arrives in a city "engulfed by new construction" that mimics Senal's "corporate mega-complexes" (44, 48). These urban areas were once controlled by Aramen's original inhabitants, a population of sentient trees called Dirijhi, somewhat akin to J. R. R. Tolkien's Ents. As Kitra, an Aramenian-born Hormling, tells Figg, Malin "long ago conceded that the trees actually own the planet, but since nobody intends to let them run the show here," the ruling classes from Senal "pay a huge indemnity for use of the world, a royalty on nearly everything that's made or sold or imported" (96). This has promoted an industrialism that has increased city sizes and that has driven the Dirijhi primarily to a preserve known as the "Greenwood," a form of reservation or ghetto (65).[13] In an initiative to break free, the Dirijhi join with Aramenian-born colonists in an "independence movement" to declare war on the Hormling and Erejhen ruling classes and on their "whole trade system," just as Figg and his entourage arrive (49). To improve Senal, then, Malin sacrifices Aramen through her seemingly cautious reforms, and this sacrifice leads to the Aramenians' understandable counteraggression.

Grimsley describes the opening salvos of the Aramenians' uprising through a series of news flashes, set apart from the main text by unique color and type and the use of numbered paragraphs, a satirized form of twenty-four-hour U.S. news bulletins, revised to be less repetitious and more informative so as to progress the narrative. He uses this form to describe the Dirijhi's ecological attacks: "a tree root twisting through a cadaver in a busy street . . . a large, empty retail space lay in ruins and the tree rose out of it" and "a fungus that ate electronics and their attendant organics" (51–52). The seeming objectivity of these numbered news reports imitates the relatively indifferent presentations of many U.S. media reports on worldwide violence influenced by U.S. economic and military forces. Simultaneously, these brief news flashes gloss over the diverse reasons that the Dirijhi might use these attacks to counter the ruling classes' economic and cultural aggressions, such as "empty retail space[s]," and to reclaim the increasingly overcrowded and overbuilt environments that facilitate this imperialism.

This formal innovation allows Grimsley to evoke how an allegedly impartial but actually self-interested politics can qualify any authority's best intentions in a destructively immoral fashion, even to the extent of condoning slavery. Malin, for example, exhibits a misguided impartiality like that of the newscasters. In *The Ordinary,* she worked to prevent the Hormling's economic invasion of Irion, yet in *The Last Green Tree* her government allows the destruction of Aramen at the expense of the Dirijhi's quality of life in order to improve Senal, now an Erejhen colony. Yet Grimsley scarcely presents the Dirijhi as innocent victims, as they have joined with the ruling classes to adopt a slavery system that, prior to the recent battle for independence, had facilitated some semblance of peace. To placate the Dirijhi, Kitra explains to Figg, the trees were allowed to use the royalties they received for land rights to buy children, each of whom became a "symbiont, a human adapted for life as part of its tree host": "Symbionts were the means by which the Hormling had established contact with the sentient trees and the inducement they had used to convince the trees to allow Hormling colonists onto the planet" (56–57). Ostensibly the mobile symbionts are collaborators with their hosts, the rooted trees. Symbionts, however, as Kitra realizes after her brother becomes one, serve "as slaves to their hosts more often than as partners" (57). An ostensibly well-intentioned collaboration, in part allowed by Malin in her attempt to improve life for all her subjects, turns into captivity that temporarily benefits the Dirijhi, Erejhen, and Hormling ruling classes but not the symbionts themselves.

Ironically, then, by collaboratively coopting willing participants through social and economic coercion disguised as volunteerism, the Hormling, Erejhen, and Dirijhi ruling classes re-create a class analogous to the one that lived in Senal's despised Reeks, only now on Aramen. The decision to become a symbiont is nominally voluntary, but, as Kitra reports, her brother "saw a lot of vids," propagandistic videos, suggesting that "living with the trees, having them talk" to you, was worthwhile, so he begged to join them. Knowing that a tree pays a bounty, "the price of a small farm" for each child, her parents allowed him to do so. As Kitra remarks, the "money is coercion" as it encourages poor parents essentially to sell their children into slave labor (96). In many ways, Grimsley constructs this process as an allegory to critique national policies that lessen domestic wealth gaps but only by displacing poverty onto less immediately apparent or less proximate people. By doing so, he explores the psychological and financial manipulations that encourage underprivileged individuals to turn viciously against one another, selling one another into bondage, and against future generations, rather than against the ruling classes. He particularly explores how this coercion convinces the relatively powerless that by further disenfranchising themselves and their descendants, they are pursuing a self-enhancing path.

The Dirijhi further undermine their own moral ground, based initially on ecological conservation and a desire for self-preservation to which Grimsley himself seems sympathetic, by collaborating with the followers of the massively destructive god Rao. To overthrow Malin's government, the Dirijhi join forces with Rao, who uses a language analogous to YY's Wyyvisar, although formed more narrowly on mathematical equations than on sung words. Rao and his collaborators use this language to cause extensive destruction, such as using roots to tear through Hormling and Erejhen bodies and commercial urban buildings, as described in the news reports quoted earlier. While this occurs on a global scale throughout the novel, Grimsley intensifies the violence by describing Rao followers' treatment of Keely. Rescued from the Reeks by Figg, whose own class is ironically predicated on maintaining these same slums where children are starved, "pimped to adults for money or food," and beaten, among other horrors, Keely now finds himself consistently tortured by his nanny, Nerva, a follower of Rao disguised as an Erejhen woman (107). Having discovered that Keely has an especially gifted understanding of mathematics, she persuades Figg to hire her as a nanny and secretly trains Keely in Rao's language so that Keely might serve Rao (170). Nerva, meanwhile, tortures Keely for sheer spite, causing him such pain in one instance that "he lost control of his legs, of his bladder, pissed himself and lay prone on the carpet" (24). There is a strain of child abuse that runs through many of Grimsley's novels, as we have seen in *Winter Birds, My Drowning,* and *Dream Boy,* and this inevitably serves as an especially shocking means to condemn the socioeconomic or religious circumstances that facilitate such cruelty against relatively helpless individuals and to condemn how this persists under the willingly ignorant gaze of those in power.

Rao's followers and Rao himself, however, exhibit a uniquely cold and inhuman destructiveness as they torture and kill without attempting to improve the lives of any particular population, not even their own or those of their ostensible partners. Nerva's torture of Keely illustrates this tendency, as torturing him does not increase his math skills or his usefulness to Rao. Analogously, one follower of Rao reports, "we have no friends or enemies" (166). This alienation, presumably, is why they kill so indiscriminately, including their supposed allies, the Dirijhi, who come to regret their self-destructive collaboration with Rao (294). This collaboration illustrates how a political and cultural movement can undermine its remaining moral goals and even its survival by aligning itself with an irrationally violent ally.

While Grimsley uses Rao to critique the Dirijhi's tactics as they pursue self-determination and survival, he also uses Rao to force a reassessment of YY that questions the required loyalty of mortals to an unsympathetic, even dangerous, deity. With Rao killing billions of Erejhen, Hormling, and other peoples, Irion seeks the YY-Sisters, his former teachers, to discover "how to fight" this god (271). He learns that Rao is one of what the Sisters call "Primes," of whom YY herself may be the first, beings that did not create the world but that have existed for close to eternity, learning to wield immense power, and beings that YY wants to imprison or to kill. One Sister speculates that the Primes "had vowed to die when the universe died" but that YY broke this agreement and traveled "back in time" to live again through space and time, which she now intends not to share with the other Primes (330, 339). As such, she has shaped Jessex Irion and the lands under his control into targets designed to tempt the Primes, who will want to live in newly inhabited places in the universe with lesser beings "for slaves or diversion" (341, 342). Jessex and his people thus serve as an enticement to lure the other Primes to a planet or a space that YY has secretly designed as a prison (340). Realizing that YY fostered his people as bait to be sacrificed, Irion's loyalty to her wavers, and when YY deigns to meet him he refuses to accept her indoctrination, to idolize her as a god not to be questioned or studied critically. Indeed, Irion's attempt to investigate her nature infuriates YY, particularly when he refuses to call her power magic and insists on calling it "science." This term indicates his belief that her power might someday be more comprehensible to his people and is likely not unique to herself or completely hers to gift. His decision to seek knowledge of YY rather than to fight Rao for her without understanding why also suggests his insistence on a relative independence based on the need for an informed faith. Irion's dubious faith, as YY realizes, questions her right to fashion billions of individuals into bait to be tortured, enslaved, and destroyed (352). Her decision to torture Irion because of his independence until he has died in agony indicates that she has come to view him as a threat, no matter how small (353). This murder also raises the question of whether such a callously cruel being has any right to moral authority over even the people that it itself created.

Consequently, if *The Ordinary* ends with a hopeful faith in a beneficent divinity, *The Last Green Tree* ends with a critique of the moral foundations of religion and of self-proclaimed deities in conjunction with a reluctant emphasis on humanity's need to define its own conceptions of justice. As Rao commits violent genocide, he claims to Irion that YY herself has done likewise, that she is a betrayer who has "killed her trillions," in addition to her alleged betrayal of her agreement with the Primes (90). YY's torture of Irion because of his attempt to understand the historical and contemporary reasons for going to war against Rao seems to substantiate Rao's claims about her by providing evidence of her cruelty. YY shows herself to be a being as unworthy of worship as Rao himself. Of course, there may have existed an original deity prior to the Primes, but its existence remains conjectural and so distant as to be almost irrelevant. What remains, then, is for individuals to seek their own path by questioning assumptions and by questioning seemingly sacred traditions, as well as by reforming violent and self-destructively coercive trajectories. Grimsley explores the difficulties of such reflection and self-improvement by showing the paths taken by leaders such as Kirith Kirin, Irion, and Malin. Through their qualified successes and their frequent failures, these characters critique their understandings of themselves and the world around them in an attempt to protect and improve lives other than their own. As such, they provide both a warning and a successful model for others. Grimsley thereby ends *The Last Green Tree* and, for the present, the series by advocating through allegory for a cautious hope or faith in humanity and in human constructions, rather than in gods or in a distant, inaccessible creator.

Conclusion

Throughout the diverse genres in which Jim Grimsley writes, several key points consistently emerge across the unique themes and the tailored styles of his work. He insists on a pragmatic optimism, on a need to critique received traditions so as to understand and to improve them, and on a recognition of the values and struggles of those members of society who too often get overlooked. In doing so, he depicts the hardships of rural poverty, which facilitate physical, psychological, and emotional abuse, and he depicts the difficult pleasures that come from surviving these circumstances in part through luck and in part through hard work, education, and fortitude. Interwoven with these themes, he also explores the difficulties and the pleasures in coming to terms with same-sex, same-gender relationships across a variety of geographies, time periods, and socioeconomic circumstances. Throughout his novels, plays, and nonfiction, he profitably examines from different angles the ways in which history, environment, and intentions can shape multifaceted mergers of pleasure and of pain and can shape individuals' fluctuating responses to them. These responses, he suggests, ultimately inform people's understandings of and relationships to faith and to communities. His work persistently and diversely embraces a spiritual faith, consistently rejecting institutionally mandated dogma while emphasizing the need for a secular morality that guides socioeconomic, emotional, and sexual interactions. This secular morality, in Grimsley's worlds, frequently leads to a difficult and evolving compassion for those who pursue unconventional desires that do not unduly impinge upon the desires, the dignities, and the comfort of others.

Understanding how Grimsley enhances these themes through a complex and diverse array of forms and styles enhances the challenges and the pleasures of his work. From his avant-garde dramas to his wide-ranging narrative points of view to his play with parallel chronologies through verb tenses, Grimsley uses formal and stylistic innovations to demonstrate how perceptions of pain and pleasure and the past, the present, and the future are reciprocally influential rather than exclusive or discrete. In playing with genres, variously engaging fantasy and science fiction conventions or blurring boundaries between memoir and autobiographical fiction, Grimsley draws on architectural references, on popular and scholarly historicism, and on abrupt perspectival shifts in his narration to suggest not only that the past can help us to interpret the present but that the inverse is equally true: we can look to the present to gain insight into our changing understanding of the past. Throughout his writing, Grimsley describes worlds and perceptions of these worlds in perpetual motion, and in doing so he formulates strategies for countering forces of violence and of abuse to establish an intensely valuable, if never quite perfect, peace.

NOTES

Chapter 1: Understanding Jim Grimsley

1. John L. Myers, "Breaking the Rules," *Lambda Book Report* 4.12 (September/October 1995), 6.

2. Myers, "Breaking the Rules," 7.

3. Allison, "Introduction," x.

4. Grimsley, *How I Shed My Skin,* 68.

5. Grimsley, *How I Shed My Skin,* 67–68.

6. Quoted in Lisa Howorth, "Jim Grimsley: Tales of Southern Courage," *Publishers Weekly* 15 (November 1999), 39–40.

7. Grimsley, *How I Shed My Skin,* 68.

8. Grimsley's mother at various times ran a small store and worked as a waitress: Grimsley, *How I Shed My Skin,* 110, 212.

9. Grimsley, *How I Shed My Skin,* 242.

10. Quoted in Rasmussen, "'The Story I'm Telling Is Personal,'" n.p.

11. Howorth, "Jim Grimsley," 39–40; Grimsley, *How I Shed My Skin,* 242, 243.

12. Quoted in "Writer Relives Trauma of His Youth in Book," (Durham, N.C.) *Herald-Sun,* 17 April 1995, C5; Schumock, "Jim Grimsley," 152.

13. Schumock, "Jim Grimsley," 154.

14. Quoted in Robert Dahlin, Charles Hix, Margaret Sanborn, and Bob Summer, "Who We Are," *Publishers Weekly* 243:40 (30 September 1996): 44.

15. Grimsley, *How I Shed My Skin,* 69.

16. Grimsley, "Myth and Reality," 232.

17. Grimsley, *How I Shed My Skin,* 27.

18. Grimsley, *How I Shed My Skin,* 198.

19. Grimsley, *How I Shed My Skin,* 236.

20. Grimsley, *How I Shed My Skin,* 18, 21.

21. Grimsley, *How I Shed My Skin,* 61.

22. Grimsley, *How I Shed My Skin,* 211.

23. Quoted in Rasmussen, "'The Story I'm Telling,'" n.p.

24. Grimsley, *How I Shed My Skin,* 61, 160.

25. Grimsley, *How I Shed My Skin,* 67, 69.

26. Grimsley, "Myth and Reality," 230.

27. Grimsley, "Myth and Reality," 232.

28. Grimsley, "Myth and Reality," 232; Grimsley, *How I Shed My Skin,* 68.

29. "Writer Relives," C5; Freeman, "Grimsley," 275.

30. Tray Butler, "Art of Darkness," *Creative Loafing,* 2 April 2002 (http://www.clatl.com/news/article/13007795/art-of-darkness), n.p.; Schumock, "Jim Grimsley," 147.

31. Grimsley, "Myth and Reality," 233.

32. Madden, "A Conversation," 14; Grimsley, "Myth and Reality," 232.

33. Grimsley, "Myth and Reality," 233; Canning, "Jim Grimsley," 115.

34. Grimsley, "Myth and Reality," 233, 234, 235.

35. Grimsley, "Myth and Reality," 235.

36. Ricketts, "Jim Grimsley," 327; Brooks, "Jim Grimsley," 296.

37. Curt Holman, "Jim Grimsley's *Mr. Universe* Pumps Up Theatrical Decadence," *Creative Loafing,* 7 June 2011, 28.

38. Quoted in Holman, "Jim Grimsley's *Mr. Universe,*" 28.

39. Quoted in Robert Trussell, "'Borderland' Creator Jim Grimsley Thrives in the Role of Playwright," *Kansas City Star,* 12 April 2009, 1 FYI, F1.

40. Canning, "Jim Grimsley," 119, 126.

41. Canning, "Jim Grimsley," 117.

42. Allison, "Introduction," ix.

43. Canning, "Jim Grimsley," 115.

44. Chris Freeman, "Governed by Other Laws," *Harvard Gay & Lesbian Review* 3.2 (1 April 1996), 42–43; David Ebershoff, *Chicago Review* (review of Grimsley's *Dream Boy*) 42.1 (1996), 89–91.

45. Richard Christiansen, "Romantic 'Dream Boy' Reclaims Its Special Place," *Chicago Tribune,* 7 October 1998, Arts Watch 2; Brooks, "Jim Grimsley," 296.

46. Canning, "Jim Grimsley," 115–16.

47. Randall Kenan, "White Like Him," *New York Times Sunday Book Review,* 7 June 2015, BR26.

48. King, *A Southern Renaissance: The Cultural Awakening of the American South, 1930–1955* (New York: Oxford University Press, 1980), ix; see also, for example, Trudier Harris, *The Scary Mason-Dixon Line: African American Writers and the South* (Baton Rouge: Louisiana State University Press, 2009), especially her chapters "Fear of Manhood in the Wake of Systematic Racism in Ernest J. Gaines's 'Three Men'" and "Fear of Family, Christianity, and the Self: Black Southern 'Othering' in Randall Kenan's *A Visitation of Spirits*"; Patricia Yaeger, *Dirt and Desire: Reconstructing Southern Women's Writing, 1930–1990* (Chicago: University of Chicago Press, 2009), and James A. Crank, "Down 'n' Dirty," *South* 48.2 (2016), 157–69.

49. Grimsley, "True Fiction," 8.

50. Canning, "Jim Grimsley," 123, 124, 122.

51. Madden, "A Conversation," 9–10.

52. Howorth, "Jim Grimsley," 39–40.

53. Gibbons, "On *The Borderland,*" 129.

54. Scott Herring, *Another Country: Queer Anti-Urbanism* (New York: New York University Press, 2010), 22.

55. Richards, "Home for the Holidays," 115.

56. See, for example, Michael P. Bibler, *Cotton's Queer Relations: Same-Sex Intimacy and the Literature of the Southern Plantation, 1936–68* (Charlottesville: University of Virginia Press, 2009); E. Patrick Johnson, *Sweet Tea: Black Gay Men of the South* (Chapel Hill: University of North Carolina Press, 2008); John Howard, *Men Like That: A Southern Queer History* (Chicago: University of Chicago Press, 1999); William Mark Poteet, *Gay Men in Modern Southern Literature: Ritual, Initiation, and the*

Construction of Masculinity (New York: Peter Lang, 2006); Gary Richards, *Lovers and Beloveds: Sexual Otherness in Southern Fiction, 1936–1961* (Baton Rouge: Louisiana State University Press, 2005); and Mab Segrest, *My Mama's Dead Squirrel: Lesbian Essays on Southern Culture* (Ithaca, N.Y.: Firebrand, 1985).

57. Dahlin et al., "Who We Are," 44.

58. Howorth, "Jim Grimsley," 39–40; Grimsley, *How I Shed My Skin,* 5.

59. Canning, "Jim Grimsley," 121–22; Richards, "Muscle Men," 73, 74.

60. Canning, "Jim Grimsley," 127.

61. Schumock, "Jim Grimsley," 150.

62. Schumock, "Jim Grimsley," 150.

63. Drew Limsky, "Boys and Boys Together," *Washington Post,* 8 October 1995, M9; Ebershoff, *Chicago Review,* 90; Fred Chappell, "Chances for Survival," (Raleigh, N.C.) *News and Observer,* 3 September 1995, G4.

64. Hermes, "The Ability to Imagine," n.p.

Chapter 2: The Tote-Crell Narratives

1. Allison, "Introduction," ix.

2. Allison, "Introduction," x.

3. Rigaud, "The Representation of Violence," 37.

4. Garrett, "A Voice for the Voiceless," 65, and Trušník, "Memories of Child Abuse in Jim Grimsley's Dan Crell Trilogy," 53, have both, for instance, referred to *Winter Birds, My Drowning,* and *Comfort and Joy* as a "trilogy."

5. Quoted in Lisa Howorth, "Jim Grimsley: Tales of Southern Courage," *Publishers Weekly* 15 (November 1999), 39.

6. Critics have suggested that this young boy is likely Grimsley's "younger self" or the narrator's "younger self": see, respectively, Madden, "Dream Boy: Jim Grimsley's Gothic Gospel," 115, and Hermes, "The Ability to Imagine," n.p. Grimsley supports these interpretations both through his acknowledgment that *Winter Birds* is "autobiographical" fiction and through his remark that he uses the second-person present tense because it "implied a version of Danny that had aged beyond that eight-year-old boy" whom the narrator addresses; quoted in Canning, "Jim Grimsley," 122, 125. Yet, while these interpretations are convincing, it is important not to forget that the "you" here maintains a somewhat distinct identity throughout the text, which adds to the complexity of the second-person present-tense narrative. Grimsley has discussed the ostensible evolution from anonymity to the specificity of the "you" in *Winter Birds,* noting that he came to the "second person through poetry, basically—where the poet would address an unnamed 'you,'" not necessarily referring to someone related to the narrator or to the author; quoted in Canning, "Jim Grimsley," 125. Grimsley likewise observed that in *Winter Birds* he wanted "to take adult readers and . . . place them inside that child's mind, almost to the point that they *become* the child. The reader is accused by this very subtle voice of being 'you' and that tends to place him or her in the book, and that's what I wanted"; Schumock, "Jim Grimsley," 148.

7. Bobjay's experience very closely echoes that of Grimsley's father; see Grimsley, *How I Shed My Skin,* 67–68.

8. Agee somewhat pompously imagines his and Evans's arrogance in the endeavor and the fear and frustration of a rural woman whose family will be photographed by Evans in *Let Us Now Praise Famous Men* (Boston: Houghton Mifflin, 1988), 321–23.

9. Madden, "Dream Boy," 113, 114.

10. Rigaud, "The Representation of Violence," 39.

11. Michael Newton, "Rescued from Time," *Times Literary Supplement*, 2 July 1999, 21.

12. See, for example, Randall Kenan, *A Visitation of Spirits* (New York: Grove Press, 1989); L. Lamar Wilson, *Sacrilegion* (Durham, N.C.: Carolina Wren Press, 2013); Lisa C. Moore, *Does Your Mama Know?: An Anthology of Black Lesbian Coming Out Stories* (Washington, D.C.: RedBone Press, 1997); Alexis De Veaux, *Yabo* (Washington, D.C.: RedBone Press, 2014).

13. Grimsley has noted, "in my early years I was reluctant to write black characters into my work because I did not want to be seen as attempting to speak on behalf of black people"; quoted in Rasmussen, "'The Story I'm Telling Is Personal,'" n.p. Despite this reluctance, Grimsley was careful to include black Southerners in his novels, and he attempted to depict these characters with an abundance of respect even if his caution limited his engagement with them.

14. Grimsley, *How I Shed My Skin*, 88, 87.

15. Canning, "Jim Grimsley," 117; Richards, "Muscle Men," 77.

16. The "deep green veil" Grimsley describes outside Dan and Ford's house at the beginning of *Comfort and Joy* revisits and revises the harsher pastoral openings of *Winter Birds* and *My Drowning*, an interpretation bolstered by Grimsley's observation that for adults the "shade trees" in urban "backyards" that "block out the sight" of the city serve as reminders of childhood rural environments; see Grimsley, "Myth and Reality," 230.

17. Richards, "Home for the Holidays," 9.

Chapter 3: *Dream Boy*

1. Canning, "Jim Grimsley," 120.

2. Cleland McAfee, "Near to the Heart of God," in *Hymns, Psalms, and Spiritual Songs*, ed. LindaJo McKim (Louisville, Ky.: Westminster John Knox Press, 1990), 527.

3. Crowell, "The Dandy Unmasked," 186.

4. See Michael Bibler, *Cotton's Queer Relations: Same-Sex Intimacy and the Literature of the Southern Plantation, 1936–68* (Charlottesville: University of Virginia Press, 2009), 2.

5. Madden, "Dream Boy: Jim Grimsley's Gothic Gospel," 117.

6. Madden, "A Conversation," 16.

7. Authors and critics have long used gothic tropes to evoke expansive connections between repressed queer desires that erupt in violent ways and aggressive suppressions relating to diverse constructions of power and of powerlessness, often defined in ideological terms of domesticity, socioeconomic class, nationality, race, and the reappearance in the present of conservatively denied past transgressions. See, for instance, George Haggerty, *Queer Gothic* (Urbana: University of Illinois Press, 2006), 2–3, and William Hughes and Andrew Smith, "Introduction: Queering the Gothic," in *Queering the Gothic*, ed. William Hughes and Andrew Smith (Manchester: Manchester University Press, 2009), 1–2. For explorations of these themes in the southern gothic tradition in which Grimsley takes part, see Brian Norman, "When Dead Men Talk: Emmett Till, Southern Pasts, and Present Demands," *Undead Souths: The Gothic and Beyond in Southern Literature and Culture* (Baton Rouge: Louisiana State University Press, 2015), 145, and Wade Newhouse, "'More Dead Than Living': Randall Kenan's Monstrous Community," in *Undead Souths: The Gothic and Beyond in Southern Literature and Culture*, ed. Eric Gary Anderson, Taylor Hagood, and Daniel Cross Turner (Baton Rouge: Louisiana State University Press, 2015), 236–38.

8. Quoted in John L. Myers, "Breaking the Rules," *Lambda Book Report* 4.1 (September/October 1995), 7.

9. For interpretations suggesting that Burke "murder[s]" Nathan, see Crowell, "The Dandy Unmasked," 187, and Madden, "Dream Boy: Jim Grimsley's Gothic Gospel," 112. Conversely, for an interpretation that Burke less tragically "knock[s]" Nathan "unconscious," see Palmer, "Place and Space," 115.

10. Madden, "Dream Boy: Jim Grimsley's Gothic Gospel," 112.

11. Madden, "A Conversation," 18.

12. Palmer, "Place and Space," 111.

Chapter 4: Cities and Suburbs

1. See Richards, "Jim Grimsley," 170; Schumock, "Jim Grimsley," 147.

2. For a brief history of *Mr. Universe*'s productions in Atlanta, see Curt Holman, "Jim Grimsley's *Mr. Universe* Pumps Up Theatrical Decadence," *Creative Loafing,* 7 June 2011, 28. The play has also been performed in cities such as New York, New Orleans, Los Angeles, and Seattle.

3. Linney, "On *Mr. Universe,*" 1.

4. Grimsley has called *Mr. Universe* "an homage" to Williams: quoted in Richards, "Muscle Men," 73.

5. Quoted in Holman, "Jim Grimsley's *Mr. Universe,*" 28.

6. Bruckner, "Psychological Terror, in 'Mr. Universe,'" *New York Times,* 3 April 1988, 49.

7. Quoted in Misha Berson, "Muscle Mania—Grimsley's 'Mr. Universe' Inspired by Big Easy," *Seattle Times,* 7 April 1995, H28.

8. For discussions of the French Quarter's cautiously growing queer community in the second half of the twentieth century, see Scott Ellis, *Madame Vieux Carré: The French Quarter in the Twentieth Century* (Jackson: University of Mississippi Press, 2010), 168; Richard Campanella, *Bourbon Street: A History* (Baton Rouge: Louisiana State University Press, 2014), 186, 246; and Lawrence Knopp, "Gentrification and Gay Neighborhood Formation in New Orleans: A Case Study," in *Homo Economics: Capitalism, Community, and Lesbian and Gay Life,* ed. Amy Gluckman and Betsy Reed (New York: Routledge, 1997), 47–53.

9. Judith Butler, *Gender Trouble: Feminism and the Subversion of Identity* (New York: Routledge, 1999), 173.

10. Grimsley reflects indirectly here the more politically active and overtly rebellious drag queens of San Francisco and New York in the 1960s and 1970s; see, for instance, John D'Emilio, *Sexual Politics, Sexual Communities: The Making of a Homosexual Minority in the United States, 1940–1970* (Chicago: University of Chicago Press, 2012), 187–88 and 231–32; and Nan Boyd, *Wide-Open Town: A History of Queer San Francisco to 1965* (Berkeley: University of California Press, 2003), 210–12.

11. The tepid responses by New Orleans's authorities to the horrific Upstairs Lounge fire in 1973 offers an example of judicial negligence in protecting the city's queer community; see, for instance, Ellis, *Madame Vieux Carré,* 112–13.

12. Lillian Hellman, *Six Plays* (New York: Vintage Books, 1979), 224.

13. Richards, "Mr. Williams and Mr. Universe," 83.

14. See again Ellis, *Madame Vieux Carré,* 168; Campanella, *Bourbon Street,* 186, 246; and Knopp, "Gentrification and Gay Neighborhood Formation," 47–53. In 2015, however, after the U.S. Supreme Court's decision in favor of marriage equality, many

New Orleans establishments, such as casinos, hotels, and bars, flew rainbow flags in celebratory support. One might see this as a commercial ploy except that these establishments' efforts toward inclusivity likely risked losing them as much business as they gained. Recent decades have clearly made substantial if far from enough progress toward providing the safety and equal rights for all citizens.

15. For a brief architectural history of the Cabildo, see Barbara SoRelle Bacot, "New Orleans after the Fires," in *Louisiana Buildings, 1720–1940: The Historic American Buildings Survey,* ed. Jessie Poesch and Barbara SoRelle Bacot (Baton Rouge: Louisiana State University Press, 1997), 40.

16. For a concise overview of the history of the Pontalba buildings, see Ellis, *Madame Vieux Carré,* 17, 28, and 41.

17. Grimsley analogously explores pornography as a means to reconsidering reality and coping with physical illness, rather than as an ideal, in "The Masturbator."

18. David Valentine, *Imagining Transgender: An Ethnography of a Category* (Durham, N.C.: Duke University Press, 2007), 109.

19. For a brief discussion on the late twentieth-century transgender community in New Orleans, see Frank Perez and Jeffrey Palmquist, *In Exile: The History and Lore Surrounding New Orleans Gay Culture and Its Oldest Gay Bar* (Hurlford, Scotland: L-L Publications, 2012), 71–76.

20. Grimsley had earlier satirizied a narrower range of similar themes using a form of pornographic surrealism, a surrealism based on a fictional pornographic film set, in his play *Math and Aftermath,* published in *Mr. Universe and Other Plays.*

21. Charley Stranger is an unrepentant inversion of Scrooge because Stranger never undergoes an "alteration" that makes him somewhat more generous and charitable as does Dickens's affluent Victorian gentleman; see Dickens, "A Christmas Carol," *Christmas Books* (London: Oxford University Press, 1954), 76. Stranger is analogously an unrepentant inversion of Meursault because, if the latter is "condemned because he does not play" society's "game," as Camus himself once argued, Grimsley criticizes Charley Stranger because Stranger plays his society's games all too eagerly; see Camus, "Preface to 'The Stranger,'" *Lyrical and Critical Essays,* trans. Ellen Conroy Kennedy (New York: Alfred A. Knopf, 1969), 335–36.

Chapter 5: Fantasy and Science Fiction

1. Wendy Pearson, "Science Fiction and Queer Theory," *Cambridge Companion to Science Fiction,* ed. Edward James and Farah Mendelsohn (Cambridge: Cambridge University Press, 2003),150.

2. David Tedhams, "Myths of Men," *Lambda Book Report* 8.10 (May 2000), 20.

3. Anonymous, *Library Journal,* review of Jim Grimsley's *Kirith Kirin,* 15 May 2000, 128–29.

4. Plato, *The Dialogues of Plato,* trans. Benjamin Jowett, vol. 3. 3rd ed. (London: Macmillan and Co. 1892; repr. ed., 1931), 83–90, 334, 502.

5. Myles Jackson has discussed the innovations of Chladni and Helmholtz and has pointed out that there has been a long history of "musical theorists" and "natural philosophers" who have "attempted to explain consonance and dissonance in terms of physical, physiological, and at times psychological processes." See Myles Jackson, *Harmonious Triads: Physicists, Musicians, and Instrument Makers in Nineteenth-Century Germany* (Cambridge, Mass.: MIT Press, 2006), 15–17, 118, 1.

6. See Ferdinand Saussure, *Course in General Linguistics,* ed. Charles Bally and Albert Sechehaye, trans. Wade Baskin (New York: Philosophical Library, 1959), 65–70; and J. L. Austin, *How to Do Things with Words,* ed. J. O. Urmson and Marina Sbisà (Cambridge, Mass.: Harvard University Press, 1975), 4–7.

7. For a discussion of traditional heroic narrative structures, see Joseph Campbell, *The Hero with a Thousand Faces* (Princeton: Princeton University Press, 2004), 227–28, 301–2.

8. Devon Thomas, *Library Journal,* review of Grimsley's *The Ordinary,* 15 April 2004, 129.

9. Paula Luedtke, *Booklist,* review of Grimsley's *The Ordinary,* 15 April 2004, 1431.

10. Steve Berman, "Light Fantastic," *Lambda Book Report* 13.6–8 (January/February/March 2005), 26.

11. Regina Schroeder, *Booklist,* review of *The Last Green Tree,* 15 November 2006, 37.

12. Anonymous, *Publishers Weekly,* review of *The Last Green Tree,* 16 October 2006, 39.

13. Grimsley explores similar themes of violent colonization and ghettoization and ecology in his short story "Free in Asveroth."

SELECT BIBLIOGRAPHY

Works by Jim Grimsley

NOVELS

Boulevard. Chapel Hill, N.C.: Algonquin, 2002.

Comfort and Joy. Chapel Hill, N.C.: Algonquin, 1999.

Dream Boy. New York: Simon and Schuster, 1995.

Forgiveness. Austin: University of Texas Press, 2007.

Kirith Kirin. Atlanta: Meisha Merlin, 2000.

Last Green Tree. New York: Tor, 2006.

My Drowning. Chapel Hill, N.C.: Algonquin, 1997.

The Ordinary. New York: Tor, 2004.

Winter Birds. New York: Scribner, 1997.

SHORTER PIECES

Jesus Is Sending You This Message. New York: Alyson Books, 2008.

"Free in Asveroth." In *Science Fiction: Bending the Landscape*. Ed. Nicola Griffith and Stephen Pagel. Woodstock, N.Y.: Overlook Press, 1998, 346–66.

"The Masturbator." In *Flesh and the Word*. Ed. Michael Lowenthal. New York: Plume, 1997, 241–48.

PLAYS

Mr. Universe and Other Plays. Chapel Hill, N.C.: Algonquin, 1998.

NONFICTION

How I Shed My Skin: Unlearning the Racist Lessons of a Southern Childhood. Chapel Hill, N.C.: Algonquin, 2015.

"Myth and Reality: The Story of Gay People in the South." In *Out in the South*. Ed. Carlos L. Dews and Carolyn Leste Law. Philadelphia: Temple University Press, 2001, 229–35.

"True Fiction." Chapel Hill, N.C.: Algonquin, 1994.

INTERVIEWS

Canning, Richard. "Jim Grimsley." In *Hear Us Out: Conversations with Gay Novelists*. Ed. Richard Canning. New York: Columbia University Press, 2003, 116–43.

Madden, Ed. "A Conversation with Jim Grimsley." *Yemassee* 4.2 (1997): 6–22.

Rasmussen, Anne. "'The Story I'm Telling Is Personal.' A Conversation with Jim Grimsley." *Late Night Library.* April 2015, n.p. http://latenightlibrary.org/jim-grimsley.

Richards, Gary. "Muscle Men, Tennessee Williams, and the State of Southern Drama: An Interview with Jim Grimsley." *North Carolina Literary Review* 18 (2009): 67–78.

Schumock, Jim. "Jim Grimsley." In *Story, Story, Story: Conversations with American Authors.* Ed. Jim Schumock. Seattle: Black Heron Press, 1999, 146–60.

Works about Jim Grimsley

SELECTED ARTICLES, CHAPTERS, ESSAYS, AND CRITICAL REVIEWS

Allison, Dorothy. "Introduction." In Jim Grimsley, *Jesus Is Sending You This Message.* New York: Alyson Books, 2008.

Brooks, Jody. "Jim Grimsley." In *New Encyclopedia of Southern Culture: Vol. 9: Literature.* Ed. M. Thomas Inge. Chapel Hill: University of North Carolina Press, 2014, 295–96.

Crowell, Ellen. "The Dandy Unmasked: Emma Donoghue's 'Words for Things' and Jim Grimsley's *Dream Boy.*" In her *The Dandy in Irish and American Southern Fiction: Aristocratic Drag.* Edinburgh: Edinburgh University Press, 2007), 178–88.

Freeman, Chris. "Grimsley, Jim." *Encyclopedia of Contemporary LGBTQ Literature of the United States.* 2 vols. Ed. Emmanuel S. Nelson. Santa Barbara, Calif.: ABC-Clio, 2009, 275–76.

Garrett, George. "A Voice for the Voiceless: Review of *My Drowning* by Jim Grimsley." In *Southern Experiences: Views on Southern Letters in My Time.* Ed. James Conrad McKinley. Baton Rouge: Louisiana State University Press, 2003, 60–65.

Gibbons, Kaye. "On *The Borderland.*" In Jim Grimsley, *Mr. Universe and Other Plays.* Chapel Hill, N.C.: Algonquin, 1998, 120–31.

Hermes, Richard. "The Ability to Imagine." *Emory Magazine* 75.3 (1999): n.p. https://www.emory.edu/EMORY_MAGAZINE/fall99/grimsley.html.

Linney, Romulus. "On *Mr. Universe.*" In *Mr. Universe and Other Plays.* Chapel Hill, N.C.: Algonquin, 1998, 1–3.

Madden, Ed. "Dream Boy: Jim Grimsley's Gothic Gospel." *North Carolina Literary Review* 9 (2000): 111–29.

Palmer, Paulina. "Place and Space." In *The Queer Uncanny: New Perspectives on the Gothic.* Cardiff: University of Wales Press, 2012, 105–51.

Richards, Gary. "Home for the Holidays." *North Carolina Literary Review* 9 (2000): 113–29.

———. "Jim Grimsley." In *Southern Writers: A New Biographical Dictionary.* Ed. Joseph Flora and Amber Vogel. Baton Rouge: Louisiana State University Press, 2006), 170–71.

———. "Mr. Williams and Mr. Universe." *North Carolina Literary Review* 18 (2009): 79–83.

Ricketts, Wendell. "Jim Grimsley." *The Gay and Lesbian Literary Heritage: A Reader's Companion to the Writers and Their Works, from Antiquity to the Present.* Rev. ed. Ed. Claude J. Summers. New York: Routledge, 2016, 327.

Rigaud, Marielle. "The Representation of Violence in Jim Grimsley's Novels, *Winter Birds* and *My Drowning:* Choreographies of the Body as Metaphors of Displacement for the Unspeakable." In *A Body That Could Never Rest: Relaciones entre cuerpo y cultura en las tradiciones anglófonas*. Ed. Félix Ernesto Chávez and Diego Falconi (Barcelona: Editorial UOC, 2008), 35–42.

Trušník, Roman. "Memories of Child Abuse in Jim Grimsley's Dan Crell Trilogy." *Moravian Journal of Literature and Film* 2.1 (Fall 2010): 53–63.

INDEX